WHERE TO DRAW THE LINE

How to Set Healthy Boundaries Every Day

ANNE KATHERINE, M.A.

A Fireside Book
Published by Simon & Schuster
New York   London   Toronto   Sydney

FIRESIDE
Rockefeller Center
1230 Avenue of the Americas
New York, NY 10020

FIRESIDE and colophon are registered trademarks
of Simon & Schuster, Inc.

Designed by William P. Ruoto

Manufactured in the United States of America

7 9 10 8 6

Library of Congress Cataloging-in-Publication Data

Katherine, Anne.
Where to draw the line : how to set healthy boundaries
every day / Anne Katherine.
p.   cm.
1. Interpersonal relations.   2. Intimacy (Psychology)   I. Title.
HM1106.K37 2000
302—dc21
00-026486

ISBN 0-684-86806-7

CONTENTS

To the loved ones who rest in my heart:

Sherry Ascher
Frances West
Barbara Blackburn
Jill Shea
Shirley Averett
&
The Antique Buddies
Abe (Ann Briel Weston)
Cassie (Cassandra Major)
Dusty (Karen Riggs Selby)
Jabber (Judy Burns)

And to those who form the fabric of my
beloved community:

The Admiral's Cove Bridge and Liverpool Society
Comfort Zone

MULTITUDINOUS GRATITUDE

In our era, the road to holiness necessarily
passes through the world of action.

—DAG HAMMARSKJÖLD

I give thanks:

To the Creator for blessing me with life;

To my loved ones for believing in what I could not see for myself;

To my family, who, despite various trials, showed up in time, especially Mamaw, and Papaw, Uncle Bud, and Aunt Marji;

To my community for steeping me in joy and fun;

To my clients for calling for the best from me;

For the sacred places of the earth, particularly Camp Koch, Northern Hills, Hollyhock, Delphi, and the Island;

To my teachers, especially Dr. Jean Houston, Marge Felder, MA, and Cody Sontag, MS, for lighting passages to vivid, soul-expanding places;

To Scott Edelstein, my honorable, boundaried agent, a mensch;

To Caroline Sutton, my delightful editor, who uses brush-strokes to move mountains;

To Christine Lockhart, who does the incredible, puzzling job of keeping me in order;

To Rabbitt Boyer, Computer Guru Extraordinaire, who—at midnight—rescued my printer from convulsive fits, and who says, no matter how terrifying the problem, "This isn't serious. We can fix it."

And to Laura Blankenship and Roxy Etherton, who—two weeks before my deadline when my house became uninhabitable—reached out with their abundant kindness and generosity to provide shelter and a spirit of possibility.

CAUTION

As you deal with most people of good nature, setting boundaries will improve not only your life, but theirs as well. But there are some people who are dangerous, or who love their power or control so much that a clear verbal boundary is seen as a challenge to be defeated.

If someone has given you reason to fear them, be careful about how you set a boundary with them. Before deciding on what boundaries to set, first assess your own risk. If you, your children, your home, or your possessions would be endangered by setting verbal boundaries, create a physical boundary through distance, or by relocating. If you live with or work for a person who could threaten you if you set a boundary, talk to a third person for counsel as to the best course for you to follow. As necessary, use lots of help from other good, trustworthy people to ensure your safety and security.

Chapter 1

WHAT ARE BOUNDARIES?

Pause a moment. Stand on the earth and sense the spiral of your life. You have not come to this place by chance. All your choices have brought you here.

You created this life by the people you let in and the people you shut out, by giving your time to the quests that matter and by letting hours trickle toward lesser goals, through the pursuits to which you gave your energy, by the pressures to which you gave heed.

Every decision you've ever made, step by step, brought you to this pass. In short, your boundaries—or your defenses—created a corridor through which your life moved.

What is a boundary? A boundary is a limit that promotes integrity. At the most elemental level, your skin marks your physical limits. If it is ripped, the integrity of your body is threatened. Your cells hold their shape because a membrane contains them. Your nerves are sheathed. Your brain is protected by blood and bone.

Thousands of other boundaries might also be yours, protecting every treasured aspect of your life—your relationships, your time, your home, the way you do things, your children, your priorities, your health, and your money. These boundaries are unseen, held in place by your decisions and actions.

A boundary is a limit. By the limits you set, you protect the integrity of your day, your energy and spirit, the health of your relationships, the pursuits of your heart. Each day is shaped by your choices. When you violate your own boundaries or let another violate them, stuffing spills out of your life.

A boundary is like a membrane that keeps an organism intact. It lets positive things through. It keeps harmful things out. In this way it operates quite differently from a defense, which indiscriminately keeps things out.

Boundaries provide a clear moral compass. They keep us on track. They protect the important, tender parts of ourselves.

Look at the parts of your life that work, that have integrity. This wholeness comes from the limits you have set to protect them.

Any part of your life that is not working can be improved by boundaries. Whether the organism is you, your body, your health, a friendship, your marriage, your work, or your energy, its integrity can be strengthened by boundaries.

This book is a boundary handbook. It can help you discover the walls that are missing as well as rules or customs that confine you to one place, preventing you from occupying the wider spaces. It will also expose defenses that you may have erected in place of healthy boundaries—defenses that may do a lot of harm to you and your relationships.

We all make constant decisions about how to use this minute and that minute, whether to say yes or no to that request, whether to respond to a friend's need or rest a bit. It's the little decisions that can use up our lives, that can either support or sabotage our larger mission.

This book is about how to handle the daily demands of life in a way that protects your time and energy for the things that matter. It can help you to be clearer about what to include and what to leave out, so that you can fill the spaces of your life with the people, activities, and pursuits that are truly yours.

You are the only one who can change your life.

TIME BOUNDARIES

Sarah had set the day aside to pack the kitchen. Her house had been sold and she had five days before moving day. This was the last big project. She had just this day for it because, starting tomorrow, only her evenings would be free for the last bits of organizing.

She was having trouble getting started. The kitchen was the last room to be packed before the move, and it symbolized the end of a period of her life. Her divorce would soon be final. She was leaving a house she had loved. Throughout the kitchen were reminders of past happiness—the bulb vase she and her husband bought on a wild Sunday shopping spree, the plates they'd chosen their first year together, a stack of old Christmas cards stuck at the back of a junk drawer.

Sarah put on some peppy music, drank some high-octane coffee, and started with the glasses, thinking something easy would get her going. She was right. She soon hit the "zone," packing boxes with amazing speed.

The doorbell rang. Michelle Freeland was dropping by to

see how she was doing. Sarah liked this friendly, outgoing neighbor who clearly wished to sit and chat awhile. She invited Michelle in—and soon faced a dilemma. Michelle was fun and entertaining, and she loved to talk. Michelle's talk was always interesting, never boring, but Sarah didn't want to lose her momentum. Yet Michelle had come over for Sarah's sake. She was offering a friendly ear and a sympathetic heart for Sarah to turn to. However, Sarah knew from experience that getting involved in a conversation with Michelle could take hours out of her day.

What would you do?

1. Drop everything, sit with Michelle, and talk for hours.
2. Cut Michelle off right at the beginning before anything could get started, and hustle her out of the house.
3. Compromise by offering her a cup of coffee, chatting an hour, and then graciously ending the conversation.
4. Ask Michelle to help with packing.

Any of the above could be the right answer, depending on the process you followed and the degree to which you were choosing from your own priorities.

Here's what Sarah did. As she invited Michelle into the house, she quickly assessed for herself what her greatest need was. If she had been bent over with grief, she would have dropped everything and turned to Michelle, who could be trusted with secrets and had a large, compassionate heart.

She decided, however, that she didn't need comforting and didn't even really want Michelle's help with packing. Sarah wanted to use the process of sifting through memory-laden items as a way of debriefing herself from her marriage.

She also decided not to dispatch Michelle immediately. Sarah had faith in her own ability to stop the conversation when she needed to, and she wanted to have a bit of time with this good person before she left the neighborhood.

So, she offered Michelle a cup of coffee, they sat at the table, and she got some comfort as she talked about the pain of handling certain souvenirs of intimacy. Michelle offered to help pack, and Sarah explained clearly why she wanted to do it herself. When her internal clock said "enough," Sarah leaned forward and interrupted Michelle, saying, "I want to resume packing now. You've helped me a lot and I can tell I'm ready to get back into it."

Michelle offered again to help. Sarah thanked her, then reaffirmed that it was a part of the separation process for her and she wanted to do it alone. They parted with a hug.

Getting that comfort break and honoring her own needs actually spurred Sarah on. She felt less alone as she plowed through the junk drawer. She felt that she had handled the situation in a way that protected her own needs.

TIME MARKS THE PASSAGE OF LIFE

Time is a precious commodity. We pay for another's time when they baby-sit or prepare our tax return. We read books that tell us how to use time well. We divvy out time to those who demand it, sometimes giving more to strangers than to the people we love. We don't always save enough time for ourselves.

Are you using your minutes wisely if you pass a lilac bush without taking a sniff? Are you feeling the fluid motion of your muscles as you charge from one event to another? Do you stop to look at a baby, gaze into the eyes of a dog, or watch the antics of a cat?

My sister is one of the finest people in the world. She always values individual people above all else. To her, no task is as important as sitting down and regarding whatever human has wandered into her sphere. She will abandon a task or a plan in order to connect with another. When she does this, she is adhering to her own highest values.

I am different. I carve niches for all the things I need and want to do, budget my time for each, and then proceed in a fairly orderly fashion through my plan. I love the people in my life and I make sure to create time to be with them—but I also require great gulps of silence, reflection, and time alone. I create boundaries so that I can have each experience.

People show up on my sister's doorstep all the time, and they inevitably receive a welcome reception. Only neighbors show up on my doorstep without an invitation, and they know to avoid visiting during my creative time.

My sister and I have each created for ourselves the type of life that suits us. Neither one of us wrong.

Some people have to get the chores done before they can relax with friends; others are entirely comfortable pushing tasks aside and making chores wait. One person might take time to relax before starting a project; another might not be able to relax till the project is finished.

My sister and I have different approaches, but both our lives work. *When you manage your time according to your own healthy sense of how to order things, your own life will work, even if your way is different from some efficient, sensible method promoted in a time management book.*

TAKE AUTHORITY OVER TIME

Your time is your life. You are absolutely the final authority on how you will use it.

Of course, you may choose to "sell" some of your time to a person or organization. Then that person—a boss, client, or customer—will have jurisdiction over a defined portion of your time.

Otherwise, though, your time is yours, no one else's. Ultimately, it's your life that will be used up by your decisions. No one is as accountable for the use of your time as you, and no one will pay the consequences for those decisions as much as you will.

We hurt ourselves when we give our time, the minutes of our life span, to pursuits that don't match our own values. We each need to assess our own truths around the use of time, be clear about our own feelings and values, and protect our own time needs.

People tend to fall somewhere along a continuum between the extremes of always giving away their time to never allowing for any flexibility at all. Either extreme can be a problem. Scheduling so rigid as to rule out a change of mind or the insertion of a new need creates tension and distance. Yet an agenda that collapses too easily, a plan that is blown aside by every shift of the wind, can mean that the minutes of your life are being vacuumed by the needs of others. Giving no thought at all to the use of your time lets your life melt away like snow.

Choices

Some of us organize our time, some of us do not. Some of us are flexible with our schedules; some of us are rigid. A person who looks rigid to others may feel organized and in control. A person who looks disorganized may feel flexible and available.

There isn't a single right way to be. A large range on the continuum can allow for a balance between protecting your own time needs and taking into account the needs of the people in your life. Too great an extreme in either direction can curtail intimacy, both with yourself and others. To get close to others, some flexibility, availability, and openness are required. And if you want intimacy with yourself, you must be able to protect your time for taking care of yourself, giving yourself islands of peace and nonactivity.

Good time boundaries include knowing how to create a balanced schedule, when to shift events and when to keep them, and how to alter commitments when your personal needs require attention.

Perhaps, for example, you planned dinner with Rosa and now see that you absolutely have to have that evening by yourself. Giving respectful notice to Rosa and rescheduling with her in the same conversation conveys the message that you do want to be with her, and simultaneously takes care of your immediate needs. However, to cancel or change too many times with Rosa will cause her to back out of the relationship. She'll consider you a less intimate friend because she'll learn not to count on you.

Your best approach of all would be to learn how much time and energy you can allot to friends, then set up arrangements that match your capacity so that you aren't constantly changing appointments with them. (Occasionally you might still go through with a date simply because you catch on to your own tiredness too late to change it without creating a problem. And sometimes you may just have to cancel even though it's the very last minute.)

The point is not to do it perfectly every time. There is no perfect way to balance your own needs with your desire to be a good friend. But you'll find your schedule improving if you hold an intention to be respectful both to yourself and others in your use of time.

By noticing your patterns, paying attention to the consequences of your decisions, and adjusting in the direction of balance, you'll come to feel less harried, more rested, and more available.

Now, look at yourself. Where do you fall on the continuum? Are you closer to rigidity or chaos?

If you don't mind being sidetracked or interrupted because that reflects your own values, fine. But are you giving up the minutes of your life because you don't know how to hold on to what is important to you?

On the other hand, do you adhere so rigidly to your plans, goals, and ideas that the others around you get mowed over or discounted? If you live alone and you stick to your plans no matter what, this can be okay. But if you are someone's mate or parent, then your style has impact on others.

When our use of time has impact on someone else's hourglass, it becomes a relationship issue, and the boundaries involved are more complex.

PUNCTUALITY

If you agree to meet someone at a certain time, you are creating a contract with that person. Every minute that you are late uses a portion of the other person's life.

Being habitually late starts affecting relationships. Your lateness squanders the time of the person who is waiting, and it can create distance and friction.

I know that some friends will be punctual and that this is important to them, so I am too. With other friends, we have a fifteen-minute grace period. Other friends are always late, so I'm late too.

When I was young I was often late—a combination of an unmanageable life, perfectionism, procrastination, and a lack of understanding of the effect of lateness on others. As I've gotten healthier, I've gotten more punctual.

It helped me also to realize that it is easier to be early than to be on time. Being on time requires precision; arriving at exactly the right moment requires perfect coordination in leaving, getting through traffic, and finding parking. It is easier to aim for the vague space called early.

Punctuality is partly defined by one's culture and subculture. Some cultures find lateness rude and insulting; others use time in a fluid fashion that includes a broad band of minutes rather than one point on the clock.

Even the region in which you live can make a difference. Arrive early at a party in Seattle and you'll find the hostess in the shower. Arrive late at a party in the Midwest and it may be over. When members of different cultures mix, they may inadvertently insult each other by being early or by being late.

When you are late, what's it about? Are you disorganized?

Do you plan poorly? Do you get distracted or sidetracked? Do you try to do too much? Do you leave too much to the last minute? Are you fearful of arriving, or resentful about leaving home? Do you have insufficient help with the things you have to do? Do you simply not care about being punctual?

If you are a punctual person and you have a friend who is usually late, think about what you need. Talk to your friend about how you feel, the message you are getting, and what you want.

If that friend continues to be late, you can choose to be late yourself. You can reset your arrival time to correspond with your friend's habit. You can also set a limit for how long you'll wait. When you reach that limit, leave.

Setting a boundary for the amount of lateness you'll tolerate can be freeing. In keeping such a boundary, you maintain ownership over your life's time.

HEALTHY TIME BOUNDARIES

Healthy time boundaries are somewhat flexible, allowing for the insertion of a new decision based on your priorities and your true obligations to others. They are also somewhat firm, protecting your schedule from interruptions that don't truly require your attention.

Your greatest obligation in your use of time is to yourself, so that you are filling the days of your life with the pursuits and activities that reflect your deepest values. Time boundaries protect these pursuits, creating the limits that allow you to interact most fully with what matters to you.

When we clutter our lives with imagined obligations, unnecessary activities, and distractions that only kill time, we dilute the power of our lives.

You have the ultimate responsibility for the use of your time. At the end of your life, none of the excuses or defenses will matter. What will matter is that you spent your time on the experiences you wanted to have.

Chapter 3

DEFENSES VERSUS BOUNDARIES

When Rachel Wannamaker walked into Seth Greenbank's chemistry class, he couldn't take his eyes off of her. Her hair framed her face like satin curtains. Those eyes, an ocean blue, drew him in so deep he couldn't think of anything more important than being inside them.

It wasn't courage that prompted him to invite her for coffee at the end of class. He couldn't have stopped himself any more than feathers can make themselves fall straight.

The grace he saw in her fluid gestures turned out to represent the real thing. She had an internal graciousness as well. He couldn't resist her. He fell so hard in love with her that he never hit bottom. They married a few weeks before he shipped out to Vietnam.

He never once had the slightest worry that she would leave him. He trusted her absolutely. He didn't feel heroic exactly, but he was giving up years of his life to a miserable experience for the sake of his country so he thought he was racking up credits with both God and woman, namely Rachel.

While he was keeping faith with the traditions of manhood, the people of his country were abandoning ship. The populace was so against the war, and the politicians promoting it, that many forgot to stand behind the young men who had no choice about being there.

Rachel continued to write him letters of love and encouragement, but she also wrote of incomprehensible activities at law school, such as protest rallies and a petition she had drafted to emphasize the illegality of the war he was fighting. She loved him personally, but she hated what he was doing and saw it as having no value.

These things made no sense to him. When his tour was over, he returned to a country he didn't recognize and a wife he couldn't understand. He could hardly find traces of the girl he had kissed good-bye in the poised woman who greeted him at the airfield. While he had been pining for her in the mud and terror, she had converted herself into a powerhouse who fearlessly challenged any person or institution that stomped on the little guy.

They stumbled along for several years, producing two children, a mortgage, and a suburban lifestyle. Then, after a decade of accusing him of not participating in the marriage, Rachel filed for divorce, and he was out on the street.

She had never been sexually unfaithful to him, but she had abandoned him by becoming a different person with foreign perspectives. Her mind had become unfaithful to him.

Seth was shell-shocked after the divorce. It took him a few years to establish a routine that satisfied him. He set up his own accounting business and got involved with a ham radio group. With the social activities of the ham group and his daughters on alternate weekends, his life was full enough.

Then Becky Race came to work for him. She was a pint-sized bundle of energy topped with flyaway brown hair. After

a while they began dating. He could tell that she was a boun-
tiful person, and she was obviously crazy about him. She was
an incredible cook and gentle with his daughters. After a
while it just made sense to marry her.

She continued to be the same person after he married her.
If he was waiting for her to prove herself, she came through
like the Red Cross. She was kind, womanly, generous of heart
and energy, especially toward him.

He had no complaints. She had only one. She could feel
that he held his heart in reserve.

He knew he could trust her. He knew she was devoted to
him, but he could not let his heart out of its box. He couldn't
risk the carefree, spontaneous joy of loving when its amputa-
tion had brought him such darkness. Occasionally she would
do something that would so touch him that he very nearly felt
himself open. But he would clamp down on the impulse and
harden himself again.

When Seth was seventy-eight and sat in the shadows of the
funeral home, with his Becky cold and silent amid the flowers, his heart broke a second time, as much for the loss of
years of loving as for the woman who was gone.

For many of us, our first exuberant love ended badly. We were
young, innocent, unskilled, and we didn't know how fragile
love could be. That first heartbreak laid us low. We had never
imagined we could hurt so excruciatingly and not have a visi-
ble wound.

Some of us react to that situation by making a decision,
often an unconscious one, to guard our hearts from then on.
We might love again, but never so wildly.

Similar results can be spawned by other situations. Being
failed by someone we've wholly trusted or boundlessly

needed can be shattering. No matter what age we are when this happens, it can set the parameters for how much we will dare risk again—not only with that person, but with anyone.

When we withdraw ourselves from the possibility of a repeated calamity—by walling out certain feelings (or a certain intensity of feeling), or by not allowing ourselves to repeat such trust, need, or love again—we take ourselves into a fortress, a defended state of being. Even if the original loss happens when one is so young as to be not fully conscious, a defense can still be erected.

A defense can be a state or an action. We are in a defended state when we stand behind some sort of unilateral protection in order to prevent a feeling we can't bear to experience again. Defensive actions are discussed in Chapter 5.

We take pride in our sentience, justly so, but instinct and survival have lives of their own seemingly separate from our great thinking brains. We can make a sincere decision to be more open or to let in joy—and our intention can be powerful—but if an approaching shadow looks anything like what hurt us in the past, we may fend it off without conscious thought. There are ways for us to reset this programming, and these ways are not violent, but they do take commitment and patience.

Like most babies, Helen came into the world receptive to whatever would happen. From the get-go she had emotional as well as physical needs. Being fed, diapered, and warm was good but not enough. She also needed to be held, cuddled, and embraced. She needed to feel safe and connected to another human being.

Her psyche reached through the mists in search of an answering heart, as if she had a cord that needed to be plugged in. Unfortunately, Helen got a mom without an outlet. Mom herself had a cord that needed to be plugged in. A little baby teeming with needs was not her best companion.

When little Helen ran into the house with blood gushing from a cut, Mom ran out of the house and called a neighbor. Helen got a black eye from the neighborhood bully and Mom asked what she'd done to provoke it. When she was playing with her older sister and her sister fell and broke her arm, Mom blamed three-year-old Helen for the damage (for forty years).

Helen's mom wanted to be taken care of herself. She resented Helen for presenting these pesky needs and for creating situations that demanded something of her.

Deep down inside, Helen was in pain. Needing this Teflon-coated woman hurt way too much, so her psyche decided not to need ever again.

For the next forty years, Helen went through life on automatic. She made great decisions. She married a good man, found a comfy life, and was popular, but she went through half a lifetime without feeling.

Her stockade covered extensive ground. Not only did Helen stop needing, she also blocked contact with her inner self. She felt no joy, no sorrow, no peace, no thrill, no heart-expanding happiness, no grief. She did not reach out for emotional connection and didn't take it in when it was offered to her.

As children we may opt for a defended state if our circumstances are dangerous, hostile, nonsupportive or dismissive. Emotional abuse or exploitation, emotional neglect or abandonment, lack of support for the natural stages of development—any of these can cause a complete reordering of our systems in the direction of self-protection.

CREEPING BASTIONS OR HOW DEFENDEDNESS SPREADS OUT

Let's look at a simple behavior that is a natural part of childhood—asking questions. If Franna is ridiculed every time she asks a question, what do you think will happen?

- She'll ask more questions.
- She'll ask fewer questions.
- She'll stop being curious.

She'll ask fewer questions, perhaps even stop asking questions altogether. The risk is that her mechanism for self-protection will expand beyond the mere voicing of questions to the very process of questioning. She may even resist her sense of wonder, blocking her curiosity and interest in the unknown.

We are geniuses at survival. Whatever is inside us that leads to an experience of pain, betrayal, or abandonment, we can lock away. If we get rebuffed when we seek affection, we may stop seeking affection. If we are treated harshly every time we assert ourselves as a separate and individual human being, we may fear being different except when aligned with some person or group that validates our differentness.

DEFENDED PARENTS SPAWN DEFENDED CHILDREN

Gerry's teenage years were a trial. His cold, harsh father got deeper into drink and lighted on Gerry as a target for his rage. Glen was capable of cuffing Gerry if he set the trash can down two inches to the right of the usual spot, or if he forgot to pick up a piece of homework from the dining room table.

As Gerry moved into adolescence with its accompanying agenda of rebellion, he approached dangerous territory. His father most definitely would not stand for jeans that bagged like old socks or hair that stuck out sideways.

So Gerry did an interesting twist. He got straighter. He began wearing tailored shirts and pressed slacks. He holed up in the library and became a serious student. He was burning with rage and hatred toward his father, and he turned it into a deadly competition. He would beat his father economically.

He was only moderately smart, but doors will open for determined persistence, so he was offered opportunities and he took advantage of each one. Eventually, by age thirty-five, he reached his true goal. He beat out his father educationally, economically, and socially. He had a bigger house, bigger car, nicer furniture, and a wife without dark circles under her eyes.

He could have relaxed at that point. He could have enjoyed the life he had built. He did not. Rage and hatred still fueled him, and he defended himself from both his own internal violence and the ancient violence of his father by continuing the race, by working obscene hours that caused him to miss the growth of his children, by tricky manipulations that cut off competitors at the knees. He did a lot of damage in the name of profit, long after he had any need to worry about the bottom line.

Samuel had a very similar father. He too had no room within his home to become a separate person, but he made different choices. His internal furnace also burned rage, but deep down he felt little and weak, even when his muscles bulged out an extra large T-shirt. He aligned himself with a group of bullies and became one too. Together they harassed obvious weaklings such as innocent girls; lone, younger males of other races; and inexperienced teachers. He got nervous when he was alone, so he spent all waking hours with his gang.

As an adult, he continued to cleave to one group of men or another, eventually settling with a bunch of drinking buddies at the bar. He still stoked his rage and he still felt helpless, and he bullied his wife and son.

Gerry and Samuel caused different types of harm, but harm they did. Their efforts to protect themselves from being bullied went beyond blocking positive experience and sabotaging intimacy. They also turned their anger against others.

Gerry's damage was more subtle and global. He'd make a decision and thirty families would lose their homes. Samuel's damage was local and obvious. He terrorized his wife and child, and an occasional teenager with a beating or a rape. Neither man understood the roots of his rage nor the extent of the ruin it caused others.

BOUNDARIES FOR THE DEFENDED PERSON

You can set boundaries to protect yourself from another person's defended state. Before deciding on what type of boundaries to set, first assess your own risk. Some defended people are dangerous: they defend themselves by attacking others. If you, your children, your home, or your possessions would be endangered by setting verbal boundaries, that in itself tells you a great deal. If it is not safe for you to speak to someone, you can have little hope of working out a healthy relationship with this person. Create a physical boundary—through distance or by relocating—and insist on genuine, sustained change and proof of rehabilitation before you'll consider putting yourself in their range again.

No matter how bad someone else's childhood may have been, it's still not okay for them to hurt others, either physically or emotionally, with a mean action or cutting remark. A person who does this is exploiting you, and their relationship with you, by using you to discharge their own bad feelings.

Some of us have a tendency to put the other fellow or our relationship with them first. However noble this may feel, it is not healthy—for you, them, or the relationship. Instead, you must make yourself a priority over the relationship. Put yourself (and the safety of your children, if any) first. Do not risk further harm. You may have to leave the relationship if you are to have any life at all.

If you live with someone who is defended against goodness and intimacy, joy and fun, but who is not dangerous either emotionally or physically, then you have more options. You have the right to confront them and ask for change. Communicating your personal limit with their defended state—along with examples of how their state has impact on your shared relationship and lifestyle—is an appropriate boundary for you to establish.

You are not required to adjust your life to accommodate a defended partner. You do not have to let another person's defended state curtail your own experience. If the other person continues to cling to their defenses, you still get to choose a full, pulsing existence. Protect your joy. Continue to choose life.

YOU ARE THE FORTRESS

If you are the defended one, therapy with a skilled professional is the fastest route to joy. There are also programs and classes that teach you to do it yourself. Some of these, particularly twelve-step programs (if you are fortunate enough to be addicted or compulsive about something), are miraculously effective, and have a great track record. (Although it is difficult to have an addiction, many in recovery come to feel grateful for it, because it has been the reason they have found a new way of living. Twelve-step programs offer a way to correct unskilled behavior and the principles taught there can be used to reduce a defended state.)

When you weigh the cost of going it alone versus seeking help with an effective program or therapist, remember to factor in the expense of time. How many years have been lost already? How many more are you willing to sacrifice?

Think about how many months it would take you to build a house singlehandedly, compared to having the help of friends and using a good do-it-yourself book. The process would be speedier still if you worked alongside an experienced contractor.

When it comes to psychological change, going it alone can take decades. Contrast that with the following options, each of which will bring positive changes the first year. With an effective program (one without professional supervision), joyous living can become a habit within five to ten years. A skilled professional can guide the way to transformation in three to seven years. Combine a good program with professional help and it's possible to turn around in two or three years. (All this is assuming you pitch in, tell the truth, and make an effort.)

How Do Boundaries Help?

Boundaries give you safety without making you miss out on the good stuff. Compare the difference between boundaries and a defended state in the following example:

Defended

As Perry walked toward the building he was already mad. These mandatory get-acquainted parties were a waste of time. He never met anyone interesting at them.

He walked in and headed for the punch table so he'd have something in his hand, then settled at an empty table in the corner. He watched with a surly eye while other people greeted each other. He saw only fakes, social climbers, and women looking to snare a man.

An attractive young woman approached his table. "Mind if I join you?" she said.

He shrugged. "Suit yourself."

She sat down. "What's your focus here?"

"Programming."

"Working with any interesting projects?"

"Nope."

"I've been studying the Norami system. It's incredible. Moves data like lightning. I'm having so much fun learning it, but it's taking me a long time. It's so complex."

"I found it easy."

She blinked. "What do you enjoy doing outside of this place?"

"Not much."

"Sorry I bothered you." She rose and walked swiftly away.

In a defended state, we may sabotage even the most rudimentary interactions that would allow a relationship to begin by avoiding others, discouraging eye contact, answering questions curtly, revealing nothing, showing no interest in the other person, misinterpreting offers of friendship, and flatly contradicting conversational offerings in which the content is not so important as the effort to reach out.

Boundaried

As Barry walked toward the building he was nervous. These mandatory get-acquainted parties were great for extroverted people, but he knew he wasn't one of them. He walked in and headed for the punch table so he'd have something in his hand, then settled at an empty table in the corner. He watched the other people greeting each other so easily. He wished he was good at it.

An attractive young woman approached his table. "Mind if I join you?" she said.

"No, save me from my terminal shyness."

She smiled and sat down. It was a very sweet smile. "Are you shy?"

"I'm so shy, Barbara Walters would run out of questions in three-point-five minutes."

She giggled. It was a charming giggle. "What's your focus here?"

"Programming."

"Working with any interesting projects?"

"You bet. I'm knee deep in Y Three K."

"Y *Three* K?"

"I may be shy but I believe in planning ahead."

She laughed outright. He thought getting her to laugh would be a worthy vocation.

She said, "I've been studying the Norami system. It's incredible. Moves data like lightning. I'm having so much fun learning it, but it's taking me a long time. It's so complex."

"I love that system. It's worth taking the time to learn it. If you run into snags, I'd be glad to help. What do you enjoy doing when you aren't here?"

She scooted closer. "I love gardening. How about you?"
"I've always wanted to learn to garden."

With boundaries we need not unilaterally shut out people or possibilities. Setting boundaries gives us the option of letting in the people who may become meaningful to us.

Boundaries can be used in two ways—by limiting the actions of the people who have hurt you, and by including the people who've shown themselves to be trustworthy. In other words, boundaries prevent harm and allow benefit. Barry demonstrated the inclusive aspect of boundaries by being responsive to an appropriate opening comment from the young woman. Perry, on the other hand, shut out a potential relationship by his defended actions.

Boundaries discriminate. In contrast, defenses have the unfortunate characteristic of closing out the good as well as the bad.

With a boundary toolkit, you pay attention to actions that discount you and limit such interactions with dispatch. It's your first date with Max and he dismisses your stance about dialectical determinism. This is a red flag. Disagreement is fine. Differing opinions add interest. But to brush off your opinion as inferior is not okay. His response is a warning for you to watch for a pattern of dismissal, disregard, or disrespect. If you notice such a pattern, you can back away from the relationship or see how he handles it when you set a boundary. For example, "Are you aware, Max, that you tend to dismiss my opinions? Please treat my ideas with respect."

Before you call your rejecting mother, you remind yourself to thicken your boundary. If she makes a rejecting comment, you either make a firm statement that sets a boundary or end the conversation immediately.

By taking yourself out of situations in which you or your choices are being negated, you send your psyche the message that you are taking charge of self-protection and that it need not be on automatic red alert.

You will also help yourself replace defendedness with boundaries by letting in good people. When a friend proves trustworthy, see that friend again. Risk a little more. Notice when you are treated kindly. Pay attention when someone offers you trust. As you become more discriminating about the people you let in, the spaces of your life will fill up with positive people, and you'll have less room for the harmful ones.

Years ago, we controlled weeds on our lawns with a poison so pervasive that it threatened the extinction of certain birds. Now we have weed control that is very specific in action. We used to wipe out all the bacteria in the body to fix an inflamed finger. Now we use antibiotics very carefully. We have learned that large-scale drastic measures cost more than they are worth.

Being defended is similarly expensive. Take a look at what your defended states have cost you. What opportunities, experiences, people, and joys have you missed due to defendedness? Make a list.

With boundaries, you can protect yourself in specific and mindful ways instead of walking around armed to the hilt. You can limit your exposure to uncaring people and nourish contacts with the people who have the potential to become dear.

Chapter 4

COMMUNICATION BOUNDARIES

You have not won a person's agreement when you've silenced him.

MAKING A REQUEST

Kelly is a close friend of Salvatore, Anita's husband. When Anita and Sal separated, Kelly, though not the "other" woman, actively promoted Sal in getting a divorce. Sal and Anita mended their differences and reconciled, but Anita no longer trusted Kelly and was not interested in a friendship with her.

August 12, 1998
Anita, this is Kelly. When I visit people in your town, they ask me what I think of Anita's new home. And I have to tell them I haven't been invited to it. I know a lot of people in your village. I suppose I'll just have to tell people that you are shutting me out for no reason.

August 14, 1998
Kelly, this is Anita. I'm in the middle of a big project with a pending deadline. I can't begin to think about how to talk to you about this right now.

January 15, 1999

Anita, this is Kelly. It's been six months. Maybe I got the wrong impression, but I thought you were going to call me when your project was over so that we could talk.

January 20, 1999

Dear Kelly,

Last summer, you threatened to blacken my name in my new village if I didn't invite you to my house. Apparently you find it inexplicable that I haven't invited you. Let's review your prior actions concerning me.

1. A message from you on my voice mail telling me my husband wanted a divorce. (March 1997)
2. A letter from you to Sal saying that if he tried to patch up our marriage, you could no longer be friends with him. (June 1997)
3. Entering my apartment with him while I was on a retreat, to encourage him to leave me a note saying he wanted a divorce and no further contact with me. (August 1997)

You've made clear through these actions what you think of me. Nothing in your behavior gives me a message that I would be safe with you.

In our one conversation between those events and now, when I tried to express to you how hurt I felt by your actions, you said you weren't yourself, that your husband made you do it.

Frankly, that is not enough ownership for me to have any assurance that you wouldn't be an instrument of pain for me in the future.

Before I could sit down and talk with you, I'd need to hear

you acknowledge what you did, and I'd need to be assured that I wouldn't run into such sabotage from you again.

I'd especially need to know that if I didn't do what you wanted, you wouldn't gossip about me in my new community or threaten what I value in any other way.

Anita

March 14, 1999

Anita, this is Kelly. I don't even know how to begin to respond to your letter. Let's just get together and talk.

March 17, 1999

Dear Kelly,

The needs I expressed in my last communication to you have not changed. I'd still need certain things from you before I'd feel safe enough to talk.

If you need a review of these things, please look at my previous letter.

If you are concerned about what will happen should we run into each other in my new town—since we have so many mutual friends—my plan is to be civil, polite, and appropriate. I have not indicated in any way, by words, tone, or inference, to any of our mutual friends that issues exist between us.

I only wish you could say the same.

What is the outcome you wish from our meeting? What are you hoping for?

Anita

April 5, 1999

Anita, this is Kelly. I just got your letter this weekend. It was a mistake for me to be in a triangle between you and your husband. The rest is all fallout from that. So, never mind.

As you read the above series of communications, what boundaries and boundary errors did you spot? Can you identify the problem with Kelly's initial communication without knowing any of the preceding events?

Here's a replay. Give it a try:

"Anita, this is Kelly. When I visit people in your town, they ask me what I think of Anita's new home. And I have to tell them I haven't been invited to it. I know a lot of people in your village. I suppose I'll just have to tell people that you are shutting me out for no reason."

Kelly is threatening that she will malign Anita in her new community if Anita doesn't do what Kelly wants. This is a boundary violation. To use a threat to achieve an end, of course, creates distance in a relationship.

This is a remarkable first message, given the context. After a year of silence between the two women, this is Kelly's first communication to Anita. The previous time she breathed Anita's air, Kelly was accompanying Anita's husband as he left her a note saying he definitely wanted a divorce.

Can you pinpoint what is missing in Kelly's message? This is a skill worth acquiring as you become more savvy about boundaries—noticing what *isn't* said or what isn't done. What isn't said can be a boundary error. Figuring out what's missing can help you spot a manipulation or explain why an interchange seems off kilter.

What is *missing* in Kelly's initial message? Of the following choices, what should she have included?

1. A clear request.
2. Acknowledgment of events that had gone before.

3. Acknowledgment of the current state of their relationship.

4. Some sort of compliment toward Anita.

The first three options would have increased Kelly's chances for a successful outcome. To turn this into a healthy communication, Kelly could have made a clear, direct request, and acknowledged the current situation between them and the substance of preceding events. Given their estrangement, a compliment would have seemed manipulative and out of place.

Here's an example of a healthy way to make a request:

"Anita, this is Kelly. I realize I participated in several events that probably caused you a lot of pain. I know I did things that hurt you. I am friends with Sal, and now that you two are back together, I'd like to see if I can repair things with you. I'd really like to see your new house, and it's awkward for me when mutual friends ask me what I think of it. Could you consider meeting with me to see where we can go with this? Call when you can, please. 'Bye."

HEALTHY COMMUNICATION BOUNDARIES, PART I

- If you want something, make a clear, straightforward request.
- If your request doesn't fit the nature of your current relationship, acknowledge that. For example, if you have a history of unfinished issues with the person and you wish to establish better terms, acknowledge both the current situation and your wish for something different.
- Remember that the other person has a right to refuse your request. If they refuse, you can negotiate in an effort to find some way to honor both their needs and yours.

RESPONDING TO A REQUEST

We are not required to do whatever someone wants of us. Always remember that you carry the ultimate responsibility for directing your life. When someone asks something of you, you are *the* authority on whether or not it will be good for you to say yes.

Of course we all, in the name of a higher value, choose to do things that—though temporarily uncomfortable or full of effort—will in the long run bring us closer to our preferred life. I might not really want to sit at a booth at the county fair and talk about raising chickens, but for the sake of happy chickens and doing my part in the community, I'll put in a half day.

When someone requests something of you, consider if that's the best use of your time and energy, and if saying yes can be life-giving to you in some way. If it's not good for you to do exactly what the other person wants, see if a variation could make it work.

As practice, you might, with the next few requests that come your way, come up with a counteroffer that opens negotiation. Instead of a quick yes or no, see if changing something about the request could make it fit you better.

In the initial interchange between Anita and Kelly, for example, Kelly implied a request. Anita made a counteroffer, which was an opening of negotiation. Then Kelly let the whole thing run aground by not acknowledging the counteroffer.

Kelly committed a series of communication errors that ended up costing her what she wanted. When you look at the series of messages from Kelly, she has a pattern of neglecting to acknowledge Anita's communications.

Look at the following interchange. Notice what is missing.

January 20, 1999
Dear Kelly,
Before I could sit down and talk with you, I'd need to hear you acknowledge what you did and I'd need to be assured that I wouldn't run into such sabotage from you again.

March 14, 1999
Anita, this is Kelly. *Let's just get together and talk.*
This is manipulation by denial. Kelly's actions are saying: I'll ignore your counteroffer, pretend it never happened, and just go on with what I want.

Ignoring boundaries is itself a response. We sometimes feel that if a person tromps over us after we've said no, then we must not have been clear. We can get caught in the trap of explaining again and again, meanwhile letting the other person take advantage of us.

If you find yourself trying to educate the other person over and over, you are working too hard. Notice how Anita handled it. When Kelly ignored her first letter, Anita essentially said, "even though you ignored the points in my previous letter, they still stand. Read it again if you need a reminder."

We do not need to take responsibility for another person's refusal to respond. If your reasonable request, counteroffer, or boundary is ignored, pay attention. You *are* being responded to. The other person is responding with disregard. At that point, you are justified in setting a firmer boundary or in protecting yourself further.

When Anita set her boundary—*I will talk with you only under these conditions*—Kelly could have responded with further negotiation, but such a response would have required first that Kelly acknowledge the boundary that Anita set.

For example, "Anita, I realize you need to hear me admit

that I did things that hurt you, and I'm willing to do this, but I need to do it in person, not over the phone or in a letter.

"I am sorry I threatened you with gossip. I get impulsive, and things just come out of my mouth that I don't really mean, and then I regret them later.

"I promise to keep our issues just between us. And I can already say I'm sorry. A year ago I felt loyal to Sal, and I was seeing only his hurt. I forgot that there are always two sides, and I did ignore what I was doing to you.

"So, I'm asking you to meet with me even though I can't give you all of what you want now."

With that kind of acknowledgment, Anita could not only feel safe but expect that a conversation with Kelly might go in a positive direction.

HEALTHY COMMUNICATION BOUNDARIES, PART II

- Acknowledge the other person's request—or ask for clarification if it isn't clear.
- When someone makes a request, before saying yes or no, ask yourself if there's a way that you would be benefited if the conditions were changed somewhat.
- Communicate the changes you propose or set boundaries on the original request.
- Notice if you have entered a process of negotiation. Your counteroffer may be met with another offer. If you each acknowledge the variation proposed to you before countering that proposal, the negotiation will feel positive, and the chances are excellent you'll create an outcome that will be satisfying to both of you.
- Pay attention to what is missing in a conversation. If your reasonable questions go unanswered, or if your

boundaries, conditions, or counteroffers are ignored, that is a response. Instead of trying harder, center yourself again, remember what you want, and state it clearly again.

It's okay to point out that the other person is ignoring what you are saying. "Fred, I said I would not cook dinner for your poker club unless you did the shopping and the cleanup. Ignoring my conditions is not improving your chances. I won't do it at all if you won't help me."

COMMUNICATION VIOLATIONS

- Refusing to acknowledge boundaries set by the other person
- Refusing to respond to appropriate questions about the request
- Ignoring the other person's responses
- Ignoring the context of your relationship
- Making a request inappropriate to the relationship (without acknowledging that the request is unusual or inappropriate)

HANDLING QUESTIONS

You are not required to answer every question put to you. If a person asks a question that feels inappropriate given the nature of your relationship, you do not have to answer. (We have sometimes been so schooled in being polite that we sacrifice ourselves on the altar of courtesy.)

Look at how the same question can be handled differently based on who's asking:

From Aunt Mabel (notorious busybody who can be counted on to spread your answer—with considerable distortion—to people you don't even know):

"You're a pretty girl, Evie. But looks don't last forever. You're almost thirty. You should be thinking of marriage. Are you dating anyone?"

"What about you, Aunt Mabel? Uncle Fred's been gone a long time. Have you got your eye on anyone?"

Or, If Uncle Fred is still kicking . . . "How many couples do you know who are actually *happily* married, Aunt Mabel?"

From someone at your office who is a distant acquaintance:

"Are you married?"

"Why do you ask?"

From a person you just met at a party in whom you have no interest:

"Are you dating anyone?"

"I'll let that be my little secret."

Or, "We just don't know each other well enough for me to answer."

From your mom, who means well, but who has a tendency to put her anxieties on you:

"Are you dating anyone, dear? You know, the longer you wait, the fewer fish in the sea."

"Mom, I've got a squid lined up right now."

Or, "Gee, Mom, maybe I should rush out and marry the first drunk I see. Do you think it's better to be married to a jerk than to be single and happy?"

From your brother, who always thinks he knows what's best for you to do:

"Are you still dating that nowhere farmer, Harold?"

"Are you referring to that steady, dependable, trustworthy, honorable guy I introduced you to at the reunion?"

From your best friend, who keeps confidences and cares a lot about you:

"Are you still seeing Harold?"

"Yes, and while I like him a lot, sometimes I worry because I'm not that excited when I know I'm going to see him."

TECHNIQUES FOR HANDLING INAPPROPRIATE QUESTIONS

- Ask *them* a question.
- Turn the topic to them.
- Take their question to its extreme.
- Answer in a way that doesn't reveal any tender or intimate information.
- Ask them why they are asking.
- Acknowledge that you don't know them well enough to reveal the answer.
- End the conversation.

INFORMATION BOUNDARIES

Be the guardian of your own tender information. Be careful about revealing delicate or personal information to someone who's mean, careless, or untrustworthy. Consider the following boundary violations:

Joy Stealing

After five years of hard work, Matthew finally got a promotion. He was overjoyed. He called his dad looking for approval and celebration.

"Dad, I've been promoted to shift supervisor!"

"I don't know why you want to work in production. Computers are where the money is."

Matthew was immediately deflated. His achievement was ignored. His dad's message was, "You still aren't doing it right."

Which of the following responses would have fostered Matthew's joy?

1. "How much more money will you get?"
2. "Your older brother just made captain. You should call and congratulate him."
3. "Took you long enough."
4. "I owned a company when I was your age."
5. "Fantastic, son! Let me take you out to dinner to celebrate."

Response 5 is the only one that is supportive. All the others would have stolen Matthew's joy.

If someone has a track record of missing the point, responding critically, or one-upping you, don't take your joy, self-revelations, or achievements to that person. Look toward someone who is truly on your side.

Discounting

"Sis, I had such an important realization. I care about children more than anything. I'm going back to school and get my teacher's degree."

"What makes you think that will make you happy?"

If, after a long process, you discover something significant about yourself or life, or about what you care about, tell only

a safe person. Don't risk an important discovery with someone who won't appreciate its significance.

Usurping

"Mom, my book is going to be published!"

"Well, Talia, isn't that fine. I guess we didn't do such a bad
job raising you after all. I can't wait to tell all my friends."

Talia's mother took the credit for herself. She is going to
tell her friends, not to brag about Talia, but to glorify herself.
She is usurping the credit and pirating Talia's achievement.

If you have friends or relatives who are similarly self-
absorbed, looking at anything you say for what it means to
them, wait to tell them your good news until you've experienced all the joy of it for yourself. Later on, when you've already claimed all the juice of your achievement, their reaction
won't take so much from you.

Tell private, confidential information only to people you
can trust to keep your secrets. Sometimes really charming
people are so warm that we want to open ourselves to them.
But be sure, before you go too far, that they are willing and
able to hold sacred what you tell them. No matter how
charming someone is, if they have divulged your privacies in
the past, you risk continued exposure if you confide in them
again.

Overtalking

On *Oprah Winfrey* recently, I saw a program where a man
was saying, essentially, "Women just want one thing and one
thing only—a man's billfold. That's all they care about. If a
man doesn't have a job, forget it, a woman's not interested!"

His face was red, he was bent forward in his chair, and he spoke loud enough to reach the people in the bleacher seats. But Oprah's show doesn't have bleacher seats. Women in the audience tried to speak to him, but each time he interrupted them and returned to his favorite theme, of which the above was an excerpt.

Just from the bit I've said, can you be a boundaries sleuth and detect the boundary violations in the situation?

Pick from the following list:

1. Having a strong opinion.
2. Making a blanket statement about an entire group and refusing to allow someone from that group to demonstrate that the statement does not apply to them.
3. Bullying someone so that her voice is silenced.

Choice 1 is the only example that isn't a boundary violation. Many of us hold strong opinions. Nothing is wrong with that. The problem comes when we actively prevent someone else from expressing their opinions, especially when they are our partner in an intimate relationship.

The Discounter

Dear Steve,

We've only met twice—once as children and once as adults. Still, we are brother and sister. Perhaps there'd be benefit to both of us in communicating.

I realized, in reading the last e-mail from Dad, that he was speaking to both his children. So I looked at the list of e-mail addresses and thought Steson must be you. I hadn't looked closely at the list before because it seemed a private thing.

So, hi! I thought I'd send an e-mail message to you directly to let you know that if you'd ever like to talk to me directly, I would welcome knowing you better and what your life is like.
Kristin

Kristin,
I didn't realize SewSeam was your e-mail address or that Dad's letters were going to you also.
Privacy on the Web, no such thing.
Get to know me? I'm not sure you or I want that, but you are welcome to stop by if you are ever passing through Talla-hassee.

Dear Steve,
A person can respect another's privacy, even if the system as a whole does not support it.
I would like to know you better, don't know why you think I wouldn't, but I'll respect your preference.
(Does anyone actually pass through Tallahassee?)
Kristin

Kristin,
Don't misunderstand my last remark.
It's just that charming and sweet are not me.
As my co-workers will tell you, I'm well on my way to be-coming a grouchy old man.

Dear Steve,
Do you enjoy being grouchy?
Kristin

To: Kristin

I am not really grouchy—rather, the terms are blunt, plain-spoken. I rarely exhibit anger, and am generally in a good mood.

This short interchange contains several types of communication violations. I call two of these "billiard ball" and "hit and run."

A healthy conversation resembles a tennis game. Person A tosses a conversational ball by making a statement. Person B returns the ball by responding in a way that includes an acknowledgment of person A's meaning. Then person A returns the ball by responding in a way that acknowledges person B's response. The conversation may travel over different subjects, but each response in some way connects to the other person's previous comment.

In a billiard ball conversation, each successive comment is in a new direction, connecting poorly or not at all to the previous comment. Person A makes a statement. Person B puts a different spin on the statement and then responds to the new spin as if it were the original meaning. If person A restates their original meaning (trying to establish a tennis game conversation), person B again gives it a different spin and goes off in a different direction, bouncing off their own thoughts, instead of taking in the meaning of person A.

Did you spot the billiard ball statements between Steve and Kristin?

Here's an example:

K: *I would like to know you better, don't know why you think I wouldn't, but I'll respect your preference.*

S: *Don't misunderstand my last remark. It's just that charming and sweet are not me. As my co-workers will tell you, I'm well on my way to becoming a grouchy old man.*

K: Do you enjoy being grouchy?

S: I am not really grouchy—rather, the terms are blunt, plainspoken. I rarely exhibit anger, and am generally in a good mood.

Even when Kristin responds precisely to Steve's statement, he spins her statement and denies it. Nearly every statement on his part negates her previous comment in some way.

Such a communication style could, over time, cause a loss of clarity and motivation for Kristin. This style not only makes communication nearly impossible, it also is a crazymaking experience for her. The subliminal message from Steve is, "I discount everything you say, even if you say what I say." Kristin would need to be very clearheaded to follow the twists of the conversation and to stay on track with her original intention.

Now look at the "hit and run" statements. I use this term when a person throws a punch or discounts the speaker in some way, and then pretends they haven't or goes on in a different tone as if the barb didn't sting. It feels crazymaking to the receiver, whose head is spinning, trying to reconcile the conflicting messages.

Offer: I would welcome knowing you better.

Hit and Run: Get to know me? I'm not sure you or I want that but you are welcome to stop by if you are ever passing through. . . .

(Hit: the indirect rejection. Making it sound as if he's speaking for her though his words contradict her message. Run: Invitation to stop by if ever passing through when they live at such a distance from one another. Appears to be a counteroffer but too unlikely an option to be a real possibility.)

Offer: I looked at the list of e-mail addresses and thought Steson must be you. I hadn't looked closely at the list before because it seemed a private thing.

Hit and Run: Privacy on the Web, no such thing. . . .

(Hit: Ignoring and discounting an offer. Run: Changing the subject without acknowledging the offer.)

What do you think is the overall message when someone uses a hit and run and/or a billiard ball conversational style? Pick one of the following possibilities:

1. Seeks intimacy. Wants to be close to other person.
2. Is warning the other person not to get close.
3. Hopes the other person will come to know who they are.
4. Is really interested in the other person.

The answer is choice 2. Billiard ball and hit and run conversations warn the other person to keep their distance. These techniques block and prevent intimacy.

The other communication violation contained in nearly all of Steve's responses is that he negates Kristin's comments and ignores any positive aspect of what she is offering him. What do you think someone gains by repeatedly discounting or negating what another person says?

1. A feeling of equality in the relationship.
2. A partner whose esteem is enhanced.
3. A sense of being more right or one up in relation to the other.
4. A partner who is motivated to communicate.

The answer is choice 3. When a person repeatedly negates what another person is saying, they are presuming to rule over the other person's speech and thoughts.

The actual communication between Kristin and Steve continued through several more letters, which followed the same pattern shown here. She kept trying to clarify his meaning, and he kept spinning and negating, except that occasionally he would reveal something of his life or ideas.

Whenever he seemed to be offering her something about himself, Kristin would respond warmly and reveal something about herself, matching his level of risk. It seemed as if, despite a poor start, they were making little steps forward. Then the whole thing collapsed under another series of billiard ball/negating letters.

STAYING IN A NEGATIVE CONVERSATION TOO LONG

Let's look at Kristin's part in this situation. From the beginning Steve was giving her the big picture. He didn't want intimacy. He was suspicious of being known and saw that as threatening.

Why did she keep going? What kept her from saying, "Communicating with you is obviously going to be more work than I want to put into it. You keep changing the meaning of what I'm saying and negating both my invitations and my thoughts and speech. This is too much trouble. I quit."

Kristin did what a lot of well-meaning people do. She couldn't believe Steve was really turning down an opportunity for friendship. She seemed to think that if she just said it clearly enough, Steve would understand her invitation and want to accept it. Women, especially, seem to keep trying in a relationship after they've gotten 270 messages to go away.

In addition, we are likely to try harder when the other person is a relative. The stakes are higher when you are seeking a relationship with a parent or sibling.

We are allowed to refuse an invitation to friendship or relationship. It's easier on everyone if this can be said directly but, unfortunately, many folks communicate their refusals indirectly—by committing boundary violations. Your job—if someone is committing communication violations against you—is to notice the big picture, take yourself out of the situation, and save your energy and goodness for someone who can appreciate them.

Chapter 5

SETTING BOUNDARIES ON DEFENSIVENESS

James Keystone decided to confront his wife. He realized that he was happier when he was not at home, that for a long time he'd gradually been losing interest in his marriage. Allie was doing something that was driving him away, and he was reaching a turning point in his commitment to her.

He decided to confront her and give the marriage one more chance. He waited for a Saturday morning when they'd both rested and had no obligations.

"Allie, I need to talk about something important."

"What." Her tone was angry. She was like a cat arching her back.

"You withdraw yourself from me when I displease you, or you take something away from me, and it's starting to affect how I feel about us. I want to talk about it. This is very important to me."

"Be specific, James. Give me an example."

"All right. Thursday, last month, I stayed at the club after my golf game and got home later than usual. Since then, you haven't fixed supper on a Thursday."

"Since you weren't going to be here on Thursdays anymore, I decided to go to the dollar movie on Thursday nights."

"I never said I wouldn't be here on Thursdays anymore."

"Well, you missed a couple of Thursdays last month, too, and the month before. What's the point of my cooking a good meal if you're not here to eat it?"

"I should have called, and I'll try in the future, but," he said more loudly, "you just jumped to a conclusion and never said anything to me about it."

"You're enraged with me."

"I'm not enraged. I wish you could hear what I'm saying."

"You're raising your voice. You're angry."

He deliberately made his voice quieter. "I'm just frustrated."

"You just care about your stomach. If I'm not here to serve you, you're unhappy. Never mind that I was waiting for you those other Thursdays without any idea where you were."

"I'm sorry you were left hanging. That was thoughtless of me."

"You *are* thoughtless. What about my birthday? We did what *you* wanted to do."

"I made a mistake on your birthday. I missed your hints that you wanted a party."

"You get all caught up in your own mind and you don't hear me. You just go off in your own direction, never mind what I'm really saying."

"I did hear you saying that you missed your sister," he said, a little louder. "I thought inviting them out to dinner with us and surprising you with that and going to your favorite restaurant was paying attention to you."

"I wasn't missing her that much. You're yelling at me."

"I'm not yelling. I am raising my voice because I'm frustrated."

"You *are* yelling. You're really angry."

"Well, I *am* angry. No, I'm not *really* angry. But I'm so frustrated. You block everything I say."

"Okay, I'm always wrong. It was my birthday. I think I know what I wanted."

He shook his head. His brains were jangling. "I need to think a minute."

"You want me to do all the changing. You want it all your way. Without giving anything back."

"I didn't say I wouldn't give back. I give in my way but you don't seem to notice it."

"*You* don't notice what *I* give."

James shook his head and gave up. He raised his hands and walked away.

"Okay, walk away," she taunted him. "Don't finish an argument."

Are you tied in knots just reading this? It's hard to witness a fight like this, even harder to be caught in one. Yet couples can tangle in this kind of argument for hours, getting themselves into deeper and deeper trouble.

I'm using this couple's situation only as an example. Anyone can behave defensively in any sort of relationship. The point of this chapter is not to imply that only couples run into defensiveness, but to demonstrate many different types of defensive reactions, their effect on communication, and various ways of handling them.

Let's autopsy the Keystones' conversation and identify the defenses.

"Allie, I need to talk about something important."

"What." Her tone was angry. She was like a cat arching her back.

Allie's anger is already a defense. Of course, we naturally feel angry in response to all sorts of situations, but here, Allie is angry before she even knows what the issue is. Anger before a conversation has even started can be an attempt to control the other person. It can be a way of saying, "I'm going to try stopping you before you even start. Back off. If you confront me I'll be angry at you."

What's an appropriate response when someone indicates that they have an important message for you? To take it seriously. You may feel frightened or in the wrong or angry or concerned with your own important issues with them, but so long as they are using their energy or courage to deal with a significant matter, heads up. Pay attention.

"You withdraw yourself from me when I displease you, or you take something away from me, and it's starting to affect how I feel about us. I want to talk about it. This is very important to me."

"Be specific, James. Give me an example."

We can be blind to our own patterns. Allie is appropriate in asking for an example. Even though such a question could be a defense designed to convert the issue into evidence that can be torn apart, James is right to honor this request by reporting examples.

As we'll see, however, Allie is setting him up. With every example, she argues with him. When the responder exploits examples, the initiator will, over time, stop giving them.

"All right. Thursday, last month, I stayed at the club after my golf game and got home later than usual. Since then, you haven't fixed supper on a Thursday."

"Since you weren't going to be here on Thursdays anymore, I decided to go to the dollar movie on Thursday nights."

This turns out to be a good example. This incident illustrates James's issue exactly. His lateness displeased her, so she stopped providing dinner on Thursday. Allie's response is to miss the point and to argue the example instead of the issue.

Missing the point is a defense of misdirection. While you are talking about the trees, I'm going to pretend that this conversation is about geography. A clever defender takes a tack that is close enough to fool the initiator into thinking that the real issue is being addressed.

"I never said I wouldn't be here on Thursdays anymore."

"Well, you missed a couple of Thursdays last month, too, and the month before. What's the point of my cooking a good meal if you're not here to eat it?"

"I should have called, and I'll try in the future, but you just jumped to a conclusion and never said anything to me about it."

James had gotten pulled into the defense. He's arguing about Thursdays and has abandoned his original issue. He's now sidetracked into getting Allie to see that she jumped to a conclusion.

"You're enraged with me."

"I'm not enraged. I wish you could hear what I'm saying."

"You're raising your voice. You're angry."

"I'm just frustrated."

Allie accuses James of a feeling he's not having. This defense is usually very effective in sidetracking the initiator. In the very act of defending himself against her accusation, he starts moving toward being angry.

Anger is funny in this way. You can feel calm and clear, and then when someone accuses you of being angry, even though you weren't angry a second before, suddenly you do start feeling angry. As a defense it works like a charm.

A good response to this defense is to acknowledge the anger and then go right back to the original point. If you get lost in an argument about whether or not you are angry or when your anger started, the defender wins. *You* are now on the defensive, and the original issue is history.

For example, you might say, "I'm angry now. I wasn't a second ago. But as I was saying . . ."

"You're enraged with me."

"I'm not enraged. I wish you could hear what I'm saying."

"You're raising your voice. You're angry."

"I'm just frustrated."

"You just care about your stomach. If I'm not here to serve you, you're unhappy. Never mind that I was waiting for you those other Thursdays without any idea where you were."

When we look at these sentences altogether, we see that Allie attacks James four times in a row. Offense *is* a good defense. He's scrambling to respond to each attack. He's wearing down and beginning to see himself as being in the wrong.

"I'm sorry you were left hanging. That was thoughtless of me."

Ordinarily, it's a positive thing in a conflict to be able to see the other person's side. In this case, though, by getting more into her perspective, James is losing touch, bit by bit, with his own point. The focus is shifting from him to her. Gradually, she is becoming more powerful, and he is sliding into a one-down position.

She takes his admission and runs with it, putting him further into the wrong. Then she moves him into yet another issue. He is now quite a distance from his original concern.

"You are thoughtless. What about my birthday? We did what you wanted to do."

"I made a mistake on your birthday. I missed your hints that you wanted a party."

"You get all caught up in your own mind and you don't hear me. You just go off in your own direction, never mind what I'm really saying."

"I did hear you saying that you missed your sister. I thought inviting them out to dinner with us and surprising you with that and going to your favorite restaurant was paying attention to you."

"I wasn't missing her that much."

Allie is continuing her defense of attacking, while bringing up an old argument that, undoubtedly, has been argued many times before. Getting a partner into a tried-and-true prior argument is in itself a good defense. Each person knows his or her lines and can settle into the old rut.

Allie also introduces a new defense, one that can create a lot of confusion for the other person: she denies her own words. For months before her birthday, she talked about how she never saw her sister anymore, not since Keisha got involved in the historical society.

James took her seriously. He thought she wanted to be with Keisha and that arranging a dinner with them would be a gift Allie would appreciate. Now, Allie is denying her own words as a way of minimizing James's effort.

This is a layered defense. First, Allie pulled him into a different argument, then she used a denial of her own words to put him in the wrong. Most people would be pretty confused by now and would have lost all track of their original concern.

"You're yelling at me."

"I'm not yelling. I am raising my voice because I'm frustrated."

"You are yelling. You're really angry."

"Well, I am angry. No, I'm not really angry. But I'm so frustrated. You block everything I say."

Here is a multiple defense. She is accusing him. She is portraying him as being out of line when he is behaving naturally given the circumstances. She is also overstating his true and natural feeling.

Granted, we all have different points at which loudness seems like yelling, but we can also misuse what would ordinarily be an appropriate comment, turning it into a weapon and a defense.

James is raising his voice, true. As he is increasingly thwarted, he gets louder and more frustrated, but he is not yelling abusively. When we overstate how someone is behaving, that is a defense. The person is mirrored incorrectly, which can throw them off and make them feel wrong.

James *is* angry. In these circumstances, it is natural to be angry. His anger is appropriate. Yet she is accusing him of being very angry, as if anger weren't appropriate, and exaggerating his true feeling. This mirrors him incorrectly and is likely to sidetrack him.

Multiple defenses are like a series of punches. They are effective in creating confusion for the other person, who is forced into warding off blows. By now James has lost track of the issue he wanted to discuss.

Allie: *"Okay, I'm always wrong."*

Pretending to be victimized—entering the victim role—puts the other person into the wrong and also increases their anger, frustration, and powerlessness. Some participants might get abusive at this point, and others might feel hopeless and back off.

"It was my birthday. I think I know what I wanted."

Stating an obvious fact as if it's being argued about is another example of misdirection. James has never accused her of not knowing what she wanted. He could get pulled into protesting this. Taken together, her last three sentences are another series of defenses guaranteed to frustrate and side-track him.

He shook his head. His brain was jangling. "*I need to think a minute.*"

This is an important moment in a conflict. When a person asks for a time-out, give it. (I realize that even this request can be used manipulatively and as a way to sidetrack you, but a legitimate need to have a breather and clear the cobwebs should be respected.) Taking a recess can completely transform a conflict. Both parties can cool down, get centered, remember their original concern, tune in to true feelings, and come back in a position to respond more positively to each other.

When Allie keeps attacking and does not give James the space he needs, this is a significant sign that her primary interest is not in resolving the conflict. She reveals that she is more interested in fighting than in solving a problem or reaching agreement.

James could, however, insist on a time-out and make it happen by leaving the room. (Again, this can be used manipulatively, as a power play or as a withdrawal, but remember that defenses, power plays, and withdrawal hurt relationships in the long run, so discipline yourself to avoid them.)

"*You want me to do all the changing. You want it all your way. Without giving anything back.*"

"*I didn't say I wouldn't give back.*"

Indeed, he hasn't said anything of the sort. When someone makes an assumption or an interpretation without checking it out, it sidetracks the issue. James is now pulled into this new argument.

"*I give in my way but you don't seem to notice it.*"

"*You don't notice what I give.*"

This is the defense of parroting, taking the other person's statement and using it as if it is your own. This defense can sidetrack and confuse the initiator. In this case, Allie's statement is untrue. James is good at noticing what Allie gives. She is not introducing a legitimate issue here, but simply parroting his issue. Other examples of parroting:

"You aren't listening."

"No, *you* aren't listening."

Or: "I'm tired of being put down."

"*You* put *me* down."

Of course, both people can legitimately have an identical issue with each other, but I'm not referring to that situation. Allie is stealing James's legitimate issue and acting as if it is her own.

James shook his head and felt his spirit give up. He raised his hands and walked away.

"*Okay, walk away. Don't finish an argument.*"

This is the need to have the last word. It's hard to resist and many of us succumb to it. It doesn't do all that much damage, but it keeps the friction alive.

What can you do if someone responds to you with multiple defenses? *You can try calling them on it.* If things aren't too hot, they may be able to admit to it.

In general, refuse to engage with defenses. The more you respond to someone's defenses, the further you will be pulled from your own issue.

The first time someone acts as if they are being accused, you can reiterate your own purpose, need, or intention. Clarify the boundaries of your concern. For example, "I am saying this, but I'm not saying that."

Explain how you want the other person to receive you. For

example, "I'm not accusing you of being bad, but I am saying something important to me. You are doing something in our relationship that feels bad to me. I want you to listen to my concern."

If you start to feel confused, you are running into defenses. You don't have to be able to identify them to know that the conversation has gone astray. Take a break. Get clear again, then resume.

When in doubt, go back to your original issue. If you are vulnerable to being sidetracked by your partner, write down the issue on a piece of paper so you can refer to it if you get lost.

ONCE MORE, WITH BOUNDARIES

Here's a replay of James and Allie's conversation. In this version, James is setting boundaries by not engaging with Allie's defensive reactions.

"Allie, I need to talk about something important."

"What." Her tone was angry. She was like a cat arching her back.

"You withdraw yourself from me when I displease you, or you take something away from me, and it's starting to affect how I feel about us. I want to talk about it. This is very important to me." [Notice he doesn't let her anger control him. He also doesn't confront it, which would get him off his main point.]

"Be specific, James. Give me an example."

"All right. Thursday, last month, I stayed at the club after my golf game and got home later than usual. Since then, you haven't fixed supper on a Thursday."

"Since you weren't going to be here on Thursdays anymore, I decided to go to the dollar movie on Thursday nights."

"I never said I wouldn't be here on Thursdays anymore."

"Well, you missed a couple of Thursdays last month, too, and the month before. What's the point of my cooking a good meal if you're not here to eat it?"

"I don't want to argue the example. I'm just using the example to illustrate my point. You asked me to be specific."

"You're enraged with me."

"It's very important to me that you understand what I'm saying."

"You just care about yourself. If I'm not here to serve you, you're unhappy. Never mind that I was waiting for you those other Thursdays without any idea where you were."

"You asked me for an example. I gave you one. Here's another. I fell asleep during the sermon Sunday and you were cold to me the rest of the day."

"You embarrassed me. You were snoring like a sailor and even the minister was looking at you."

"Maybe he'll get the message that his sermons go on too long."

"You only care about yourself. If your creature comforts are affected, then you're unhappy."

"You're characterizing me as being an exceedingly selfish person. If this is your issue, I'm willing to talk about it, but not now. I'm telling you something important and I want you to make an effort to listen to what I'm saying. This conversation is my turn, my issue. Please listen."

She crossed her arms and stared at him, stymied for the moment. Then she said, "Okay, give me another example."

"Even though I made an effort to please you on your birthday, you saw nothing good in it, and withdrew from me. You were cold to me for weeks afterward."

"You get all caught up in your own mind and you don't hear me. You just go off in your own direction, never mind what I'm really saying."

"Allie, you're responding with one defense after another. Do your best to listen to me. I'm illustrating my point that, over and over again, your standard response to being unhappy with me is to withdraw and be cold or to punish me by causing something we share to disappear."

"In every one of your examples, there's a good reason for me to be unhappy with you."

"If you're unhappy with me, tell me. Let's talk about it. But freezing me out is only discouraging me from trying."

"You're yelling at me."

"You know that I'm not. Are you refusing to address my issue?"

"I was really disappointed with my birthday. A person only turns forty once. I wanted a party."

"I'm so sorry I didn't understand that. I really wanted you to have a special birthday."

"I was really hurt. Ethel's husband threw her a big party with all her friends and black balloons and black food, and they had a lot of fun."

"I can see you didn't feel special or celebrated by your friends at such an important point in your life."

She nodded. "I found a gray hair just the week before. I wanted to get some good out of getting older." She started crying. He went to her and held her. She relaxed into him.

"I didn't realize you had all this going on for you."

"I felt stupid about it. I couldn't say anything."

James asked, "How could I reach out to you without knowing?"

"I gave you hints."

"I missed them."

She answered, "That hurt, too."

"Darling, it's not from inattention that I miss your hints. It's because I'm just a man who can't read subtle feminine print. I want to respond to you, but I need bigger print on the cue cards."

She giggled and settled against him. They were silent together.

"Do you think you could take in what I'm saying now?"

She nodded. "I'll try."

"When you communicate to me by withdrawing and being cold, it eventually pushes me away. Please be angry directly. Tell me with words that you're unhappy with me. I can take your anger if you'll express it to me. Lately you've been freezing me out so often that I've begun to believe I can't do anything right for you, and it's hard for me to keep trying."

Her eyes were cast down. "I know I have a terrible time saying I'm angry. I feel angry, and then feel I don't have a right to feel it, and so I shut you out."

"Is that the only way you've been able to express it?"

She nodded.

"But it's not working for me. When I feel that nothing I do will be right, I give up."

"I can see that. I'm sorry. I think I'll need help to change this."

"Do you want my help?" he asked.

"I'll think about it."

"Who's your healthiest, happiest friend?"

"Jennifer," she answered without hesitation.

"What if you talked to her about it, and find out what she does?"

"Yeah, that's a good idea. I'll talk to her."

"I feel closer to you. I feel hopeful."

"I feel embarrassed that I've been so cold to you."

"I can't tell you what a relief it is to hear you say that. I feel like forty tons have dropped off my shoulders. Want to do something together—go to a movie, go to the park?"

An interesting thing happened in the midst of this conflict. Although Allie wasn't able to acknowledge his issue at first, she suddenly began doing what James wanted her to do. As he steadfastly held to his point and refused to be drawn into her defenses, she abruptly dropped the defensiveness and got into what had happened to her on her birthday.

When this all-important change happens in a conflict, it's very important to realize it, or the whole thing will go astray again. If you're asking for something, and suddenly you start getting what you're asking for, try to get on that path and stay on it.

When confronted with defenses, stick to your point. When responded to with feeling and openness, go with the process. If a door suddenly opens, walk through it. The chances are excellent that the other person will eventually be able to hear your concern fully. The trick is to avoid insisting on what you want while missing that it has already arrived.

Learn to read both words and behavior. Some people respond with words first and behavior later. Other people will move into the behavior you want but not have the words for it until afterward.

When you're in an argument or conflict and the other

person gives you an approximation of what you want—not doing it perfectly, but being in the right ballpark—appreciate it. Realize that the person is making an effort on your behalf. If you wait till they are perfect, you have a long wait ahead of you; they won't ever get perfect, because you aren't cueing them that they are on the right track.

So the fine art of handling defenses includes being able to discern when the other person has suddenly switched out of defensiveness and into real communication. You'll soon be able to see if this is yet another cleverly disguised defense; for if someone is faking a response, it will feel confusing to you. When they express their true feelings in an effort to engage with you, you'll sense the integrity of it.

A conflict has moved toward mutual understanding when you feel yourself softening toward the other person, when you feel like being closer, or when you want to touch them or look into their face. As your anger melts and your empathy increases, you can trust that the shift in the conflict has been a healing one.

THE STRAW THAT BREAKS THE RELATIONSHIP'S BACK

Defenses cost a lot over time. Important messages are lost, warnings are missed, and issues drag out forever. It's amazing how protective we can be of our own mistakes, even though admitting to mistakes or harmful patterns can bring enormous improvement to a relationship.

We know when we've reached a turning point in our commitment to another person. At that intersection, we may offer them a last opportunity to catch on to the gravity of an issue. (This effort will usually *not* be emphasized by a comment such as, "Pay attention. This conversation could make or break my commitment to you.")

Hopefully, if both people have worked to keep communication clear and clean, they'll have practiced the good habits that will enable them to handle this significant conflict well and thereby save the relationship.

Chapter 6

BOUNDARY VIOLATIONS

A boundary is like a line drawn around us that says, *This is my limit. Go no further.*

When someone crosses one of our limits (whether we personally set them or whether they are built in to the situation), the relationship is immediately harmed, and our own integrity can be threatened.

Occasionally a person might cross a boundary accidentally, just out of ignorance. This is called a boundary error. It becomes a boundary violation if that person disregards us when we educate them that a boundary exists.

Carla met her future daughter-in-law for the first time at a Kingsma family dinner. "Mom," said her son proudly, pulling close a young woman with dark hair and proud eyes, "this is Ann."

Carla gave a quick once-over of the girl's apparel, assessed that it was not of Lord & Taylor quality, and said, holding out her hand, "Welcome to the family, Annie."

The girl took her hand and said, "Ann, Mrs. Kingsma. My name is Ann."

Carla turned toward the rest of the family and said, "Everyone, this is Brad's fiancée, Annie."

Brad's father and brothers gathered around her and welcomed her, each calling her Annie. With each she stated firmly and clearly, "My name is Ann."

The men of the family, without exception, switched to Ann immediately, but Carla called her Annie the rest of the evening.

Carla made a boundary error the first time she changed Ann's name, but after she was corrected and she continued to use the wrong form of the name, she committed a boundary violation.

It might seem like a small thing to alter a name, but one's name is not a trivial matter. It is much more than a label. It is a part of identity, almost a metaphor that wraps up the entirety of a person. Each person's name has great meaning to them, connecting them with their heritage, their ancestors, and their history.

In certain cultures, the quick American familiarity of immediately shortening a name is insulting. To call Lord Charles Chuckie or Bud is just not appropriate. To call Habib Habby shows ignorance and lack of respect.

Sometimes we bestow nicknames out of affection. I have nicknames for many of the people I love (sometimes more than one for the same person), and it's a sign of affection; but if you alter someone's name and they correct you or ask you not to, you commit a boundary violation by continuing to disregard their wishes.

Carla's violation instantly harmed her relationship with her future daughter-in-law. The quick regard of the males of the family, however, started their relationship with Ann on the right foot. Within ten minutes, she was closer to the men than to her future mother-in-law.

If Ann had gone along with Carla, accepting a name that she did not like, telling herself it wasn't that big a deal, she would have begun to participate in her own boundary violation. Standing up for herself, even when her request continued to be disregarded, kept her spirit intact. The integrity of Ann's relationship with Carla was harmed, but her own integrity was not.

Carla's behavior told Ann a great deal about her future mother-in-law, and from that one experience she knew not to take risks with her, not to confide in her, and not to expect true affection. When someone violates one of your boundaries, or you observe them violating someone else's, consider that a warning. Don't expose yourself to any further damage or assault from them—and be on the alert for future violation attempts.

We sometimes wrongly believe that if someone has acted badly toward us, we will change their attitude by making ourselves more vulnerable. In fact, the opposite is usually true: the more vulnerable we make ourselves, the more likely it is that the boundary violations will continue or worsen.

For example, imagine that Ann, alone in the kitchen with Carla, had confided something important to her, thinking that an intimacy might win Carla to her side. This would have been a mistake, because it would have exposed Ann to further risk. She would essentially be saying, "Here, I open my gates to you. Come on in, even though you are not on my side." *She would thus be creating her own boundary violation,* because Carla had already demonstrated that she would use personal information against Ann.

Had Ann confided, for instance, to Carla that she was nervous on the way there—a perfectly natural feeling under the circumstances—Carla might translate that to the rest of the family in a way that would diminish Ann: "That girl Brad is thinking of marrying is a timid little thing. She was scared to death to have dinner with us. You'd think we were going to put her on the spit and roast her."

In the situation with Ann and Carla, Ann set the boundary and Carla violated it. Much of the time, however, a boundary is set by the situation itself. For instance, it's a boundary violation for a doctor to hug a patient during a medical exam, or for an interviewer to ask a job applicant, "Tell me a little about the company your husband works for." And it's always a boundary violation for a parent to be sexual or physically abusive in any way with a child.

Every child has a line drawn around them. Inside that space is a child's sexual, emotional, and physical safety. If a parent hits their child in the head, the line has been torn, and the integrity of the parent-child relationship is immediately harmed. If the child's other parent observes or suspects the violation and doesn't make their spouse stop, the child is abruptly alone in the world. From then on the relationship with both parents is altered.

Violating anyone causes pain and harm, but when the victim is a child, the consequences are more severe. Because children are small, vulnerable, and inexperienced, and have limited options and a poor understanding of what is right and normal behavior, they can be emotionally as well as physically harmed. Abuse alters a person's future in a negative way.

Children tend to believe that the way they are treated is what they deserve. As a result, when they are violated, they then search around inside themselves to find the reason. They come up with things like *I'm bad,* or *I don't do things well enough,* or *I failed Dad; therefore I'm a failure.* They aren't able to see that it's the parent who is wrong.

If a father deliberately runs his hand over his teenage daughter's bottom, her system is immediately shocked. Her sexual safety is suddenly gone, and their relationship is instantly and permanently altered.

Since a child is unlikely to know how to fix the boundary—and since a parent who has already violated a child is likely to violate again—the harm to the child is often lasting.

Shiree told her mom about her dad fondling her. Mom told Dad to stop, and then never mentioned it again. But Dad needed far more serious consequences than a few negative words. Mom's ineffectual response exposed Shiree to another three years of escalating abuse. She lost both her mom and her dad from that point on.

Linda, Shiree's younger sister, watched in terror and confusion as the abuse unfolded. Even though her father never touched her inappropriately, she withdrew from her parents almost as quickly as Shiree. Ultimately, the entire family lost their home as a sanctuary.

When a mother is beaten, the children are violated as well. They can't be sure that harm won't one day descend to them. They also go through agonies of paralysis—wanting to save Mom, fearing their own danger if they try. At a young age, they learn to hate men, or despise weakness or women, and their model for handling their own anger is to hurt someone.

A boundary violation within a family therefore harms not only the relationship of the two people directly involved, but the relationships of all the people in the family.

In any situation where a boundary violator is in a position of greater power than the person who is violated, the violation is automatically more serious. This power may come from use of a weapon, from superior size or strength, or from a role, such as parent, boss, minister, therapist, or doctor.

When we depend on someone else for something we need—be it a paycheck, spiritual redemption, medication, treatment, or housing and meals until the age of eighteen—we have an investment in remaining in the situation until we no longer have those needs.

Remember, a boundary violation is different from a boundary error. A boundary error is an inadvertent mistake, a result of being unaware that a boundary exists. People in positions of power already know that it's a violation to use their position to exploit a subordinate or patient.

For example, doctors already know that their position of trust requires them to stay within ethical limits. They know not to use a patient sexually or for undeserved financial gain. Ministers know they're given a greater measure of trust than a layperson, and thus must take much more care to keep their motives and actions clean. Bosses know that their subordinates will produce better work if they feel safe.

When you see someone violating a boundary that we all know is built in to a situation, be warned. You are being clearly shown that they are willing to exploit others for their own gratification or gain. Get away from this person. Don't make excuses for them. Don't give them the supposed benefit of doubt. Don't minimize their behavior by thinking that perhaps they didn't realize what they were doing. Be assured that they realize it.

If you'd rather not lose what you get from that association—he's the only doctor for six hundred miles, all your friends are members of that church, you like the work and the benefits are good—then you owe it to yourself to see if you can salvage the situation.

Muster your own personal power, center yourself, and be clear and straightforward in stating your own boundary. Remember that you do have real power in this situation. Most violators are bullies and most bullies feel pretty weak inside. Lots of times they get away with what they do because no one calls them on it.

Naming your boundary will be enough for some people. If, however, they continue to violate that boundary, you will have to introduce consequences, either by exposing their violation (telling their boss about it, for example), or by leaving the situation.

Some bullies get meaner when they feel cornered. If you suspect this is the case, then get out. When other boundaries fail, the one we can always use is the boundary of distance. We can take ourselves away from the violator.

THE DISTANCE BOUNDARY

The longer we stay in a violating situation, the more traumatized we become. If we don't act on our own behalf, we will lose spirit, resourcefulness, energy, health, perspective, and resilience. We must take ourselves out of violating situations for the sake of our wholeness.

Tariq started being rough with Chantal before they were married. He'd grip her arm or pin down her hands. Each time, he explained it away by saying he got upset whenever he thought she might be interested in someone else. For some reason, Chantal let herself buy these excuses, even though they hardly fit most situations.

For instance, there was the time she wanted to go to the beach and swim and he wanted to see the stock car races. He pinned her up against the car and went on and on about how if they went to the beach, men might stare at her and he wouldn't be able to stand it: he'd want to kill them, so they'd be safer at the races.

Three weeks later, when the mid-August humidity made life not worth living, Tariq wanted to go to the beach. Apparently the danger from roving bands of salacious men had somehow diminished.

Occasionally Tariq would leave a bruise, but Chantal told herself that once they were married, he'd feel more secure. In thinking this way, she had already begun the slow decline caused by his intimidation. She was avoiding her own thoughts that would expose his poor logic for what it actually was: an extraordinary need to control her.

They got married, and the bruises got larger. Chantal told herself he'd be better when he had a child to love. Then, after their daughter was born, she told herself he'd be better when he had a son.

It is always an illusion to hope that a deliberate violator will change their behavior on their own. If someone violates you, if they mow down the boundaries you set, they will only continue to violate you. They will stop only when *you* add some negative consequences for their violations or if you remove yourself from their sphere of influence.

STOPPING VIOLATIONS

A boundary protects the integrity of the person and the relationship. When a boundary is violated, the integrity of both the person and the relationship are altered. Your job, if one of your boundaries is violated, is to immediately protect and restore the boundary. (Exception: if you are being threatened with physical harm, get away immediately.) The relationship has already been altered, but by taking immediate action to restore the boundary, your personal integrity is repaired.

If someone ignores the boundary set by the context of your relationship—say he dances too close, and he's your husband's best friend—set a boundary right away. "Back, Jack, you're over the line." If this boundary is ignored, regardless of the reason they *give* for ignoring it, you are with a violator. Set a new boundary by not giving them a chance to get that close again. "Dance is done, son." And if they still come after you, don't hesitate to threaten them with consequences. "One more move and I'll blow your cover."

Some of us have a tendency to let people get away with things under the auspices of being nice. Forget it. The other person is not being nice. Once someone else abandons the limits set by courtesy, you are not required to stay there yourself. Protecting yourself gets to be your first priority. *It is more important than propriety or sparing the other person embarrassment.* Remember, you are not the one causing the stir. The other person caused it. If they use the social situation as a cover to get away with a violation—counting on you to keep quiet so as not to interrupt the main event—you can foil that plan by deliberately and publicly speaking out—or by doing whatever you need in order to be safe.

MULTIPLE VIOLATIONS

The boundaries around you flex and move according to the situation. With someone safe and trusted, the line thins and shrinks, allowing the other person more scope, permitting them to get closer. You don't need to keep a generous, loving friend outside a brick wall. With a potentially hurtful person, the line thickens and moves outward, so that they are kept away and less of what they do can penetrate. You wouldn't be safe from an abusive person just by holding up a piece of cling wrap.

When a husband hits his wife, it's a double violation because of her trust and love. With him she's kept a thin, open boundary. The context, marriage, has invited her to relax; as a result the damage of the blow goes deeper. If the husband then uses verbal manipulation to convince her that she caused him to hit her, it's a triple violation.

She, with that one clout, has gone from a peer to a victim, from a place of equal power to a position of less power. She is suddenly his hostage. Hostages learn to identify with their captors in order to survive, so her perception and logic will begin to side with him in order to protect her own physical safety.

This is why it is essential for someone to leave a relationship early, at the very first sign that abuse is the other person's pattern. After the first blow, say, "If you do that again, the relationship is over." And if they do it again, no matter what reason they give, leave.

The abuser is always a step ahead of the victim. The further down that road you let yourself go, the stronger your abuser will get and the weaker you'll get. They will become much more dangerous as the years go on.

SELF-VIOLATIONS

Liese loved her house. Sitting in three acres of parkland, situated so privately that she could bask nude on the deck and be seen only by hawks, it was like a physical extension of her own body, the only dwelling in which she'd ever felt absolutely safe.

After fifteen years of marriage, however, her husband changed suddenly. An undiagnosed mood disorder caused him to pick fights with her, undermine her thinking, and respond in disorienting ways. Often he was both intrusive and abandoning. For example, on their way to pick up new wedding rings a few days after Liese had surgery, he attacked her verbally all the way to the jeweler's, and she was too sick to do more than bear it. Driving to a movie, he would suddenly light into her with angry criticism. She'd set out to exercise and he'd rail at her for using a walking tape. She'd come home and find the house rearranged in a way that distanced him from her.

Nothing she tried worked. She tried organizing an informal intervention, but Eric's friends, believing his propaganda against her, wouldn't participate. A marriage therapist they tried used old, useless techniques that got them nowhere. A psychotherapist couldn't see through Eric's respectful, appropriate behavior in her office.

Liese stayed in the situation three more years. She didn't want to leave her house. She loved the view, the neighbors, the town, her garden, and her life there. She loved everything but Eric's abuse. Because she loved the house so much, she subjected herself to nearly half a decade of hell.

When we stay in an abusive situation because of some other aspect of it—a cherished social position, luxuries, wanting to stay together till the children have grown—we lose a chunk of our life. As hard as it is to pack, relocate, lose shared income, and make a new life for the kids, things do get better as a result. On the other side of all the change and work is rampant possibility. Countless men and women have found that on the other side of the sorting and boxes and dislocation are opportunity, friendship, fun, and intimacy.

Chapter 7

SETTING LIMITS ON ATTACK

Jeff came home from work feeling light and happy. He'd done his job especially well that day and felt good about himself. But Tony, his partner, was in a bad mood. He was hidden behind the newspaper from which issued growls about inane journalists.

Jeff headed for the kitchen and began putting together a pasta dinner. After a few minutes, Tony came in and said, "Stop throwing pots and pans around. Your anger is filling the apartment."

Jeff stopped, startled. "I'm not throwing pots and pans. I'm just cooking. I'm not angry."

"Yes, you are. You're angry that I took your parking place, aren't you?"

"I'm not angry. I parked in front. I didn't even notice where you were parked because there was a space right by the front door."

"You are too angry. I hear an edge in your voice."

"You hear an edge in my voice because I'm getting tense about all these accusations. I felt good when I came in, and I know if this keeps on I *will* feel angry. I don't want to go any further with this. I don't want to be angry when that's not where I am. If something went wrong for you, I'll be glad to listen. But stop telling me how I feel."

"That was an angry statement."

"Either tell me the real issue or stop."

"You can't control me."

"I'm out of here."

What happened here? Jeff came home lighthearted and in a good mood, and Tony trounced him. Tony was looking for a fight and did his best to start one. Jeff wanted to keep his good feeling, refused to participate, and, when reason didn't work, took himself out of the situation.

Regardless of the reason for Tony's anger—even if Jeff had actually done something wrong—Tony's way of handling his feeling was not okay. Even if Jeff did some dumb thing that bothered Tony, Jeff still didn't deserve to be treated that way, and he was right not to put up with it. Tony projected his own anger onto Jeff, like shining his movie on Jeff's screen, and that became Tony's excuse for treating Jeff badly. Tony thus got to discharge some of his uncomfortable feelings at Jeff's expense.

When one person abuses another, this is, at base, what it is about—using another person to discharge their own uncomfortable feelings. This is not okay and must be stopped.

This problem will not get better on its own. On the other hand, if you set good, clear boundaries early—when the person first starts a verbal attack or projection—there is some chance that the relationship will work out.

Notice what Jeff did not do. He did not try to understand Tony or do active listening. He did not say, "You sound angry,

Tony. What's wrong?" If someone is a little out of touch temporarily, this can sometimes help; but in Tony's case, with a
track record of projection and attack, his most likely response
would be something like, "You bet I'm angry. You come in the
door and make a racket in the kitchen and expect me not to
get agitated."

Active listening would respond, "Sounds like loud noise
agitates you."

And then Tony's anger would intensify.

Active listening and understanding wouldn't work here,
because Tony is not engaging in a way that would allow the
truth to come out. Even marriage counselors sometimes
make the mistake of applying active listening when a boundary is called for instead.

Can you spot the flaw in Tony's behavior that is a signal
that active listening would backfire? Guess what it is.

1. He's already mad.
2. His focus is outside himself.
3. He's hungry.

The answer is 2. Tony is not making any effort to address
his real issue, to access his own insides and feelings. Instead
he is focused outwardly on Jeff. When someone is focused on
another person, active listening will only encourage them to
continue dumping their feelings on that other person.

Since Tony's feelings are being directed toward Jeff, neither Tony nor the relationship will benefit from active listening. Tony will only get further entrenched in his belief that
Jeff is the cause of his discomfort, and both Jeff and the relationship will be harmed.

Even an understanding comment such as, "Something

must have upset you today" might have backfired for Jeff. Tony might have replied, "You bet I'm upset. I'm upset with *you*, Jeff."

The best hope for Jeff in this situation is for him to set boundaries. By rapidly erecting an energetic barrier and by refusing to engage in abusive behavior, he can foil Tony's attack. (Remember, the purpose of the attack is for Tony to get rid of his bad feeling by dumping it on Jeff. If Jeff refuses to accept it, the bad feeling bounces right back—to Tony.)

In a new relationship, *the very first time* someone tries to dump their feelings on you, set a boundary. Refuse to engage. Imagine that a force field has sprung up around you. Think of it as a wall of energy that blocks the invasion of any bad energy or feeling. Say, "It's not okay to talk to me that way. If you're unhappy about something I will listen. But don't dump your anxiety (or fear, or whatever) on me."

If your boundary is respected—if the person pivots into a direct expression of their feelings, such as, "Oh, man, I am so scared about this job interview"—then you've got someone you can work with. If, however, they increase their efforts to get you to take it, or they try to control you, demean you, call you names, or are physically rough in any way, disengage. If this behavior continues, end the relationship.

Don't take chances with a violent person. Even if they claim (or you carry the illusion) that you are the only one who understands, that you are the only one who can save them, or that your love will heal them, remember, this is a fantasy. By the time you realize that you *can't* do enough to fix them, you will have lost a part of yourself.

Don't put "being fair" to someone over your own safety, either. Many a woman has been trapped, and even killed, out of a mistaken idea that their partner deserves one more chance.

• • •

The interesting thing about good boundaries is that this whole process can work without the other person knowing what you are doing. It doesn't require a lengthy explanation or charts and graphs for boundaries to work.

Do you have a nonviolent person in your life who tries to dump their discomfort on you? If so, do they infect you with their bad mood, so that they walk in with a cloud overhead, and walk out smiling because now the cloud is over *your* head? Do they attack you or disregard you in some careless or subtle fashion? Are they nonresponsive until you start fretting and then they're suddenly energetic? These are all signs that you've absorbed their bad feeling. No wonder they feel better. The uncomfortable energy is now in your body.

The next time this person approaches you, quickly imagine yourself surrounded by your force field. Decorate this energy barrier any way you want. It can be a thicket of daisies, or your most loving friends all holding hands like cops do at a parade. Surround yourself with a rainbow or some very loyal lions. If you are feeling good or carefree or successful or competent, tune into that feeling. Magnify that good feeling. Let your confidence or joy or competence fill the space inside your barrier. Let it pour out of your eyes and shine from your skin. Then, no matter what that person says to you, stay tuned into yourself and hold the image.

In addition, build your verbal skills at stopping people who try to transfer their bad feelings to you.

"Walter, if you're angry with me, say so directly."

"Mom, I'm not joining you in your anxiety. I'm going to hang up now."

"Joan, your agitation is starting to rock the house. Either talk about what's going on or run around the block."

"My love, I can't be with you when you're doing that indirect stuff. If you'll acknowledge your mood and do something to help yourself, I'll go to the movie with you. Otherwise I'm going by myself in fifteen minutes."

People are remarkably responsive to consequences. If you create a consequence of being unavailable until they are honest and direct, they catch on.

Here's another interesting thing about boundaries: the other person may not know the cause of their own bad mood, but running into your boundary brings it to mind.

Hamish found out, when he got to work, that his best buddy, Shawn, was moving. He felt a shaft of grief and disappointment, then buried himself in work and forgot about it.

When he got home, he was unhappy with everything he saw—the grounds in the coffeemaker, the ragged dishcloth, his kid's music.

He started picking on his wife. "Maureen," he yelled, even though she was standing but a few feet from him, "can't you do something about that noise? Are you just starting dinner now? Why are the breakfast dishes still in the sink?"

Maureen refused to engage. She filled her energetic boundary, stayed in her own psychological space, and barely listened to him as she rinsed vegetables. He continued to try to start a fight, and she said, "I don't know what caused this mood of yours, but I know *I'm* okay and I've done well today." Then she left the room.

After fifteen minutes, Hamish came in, plopped down, and started talking. "Shawn's moving to Fiji."

Immediately she stopped arranging flowers and came over to him. "Oh, Hamish, I'm so sorry."

Her boundary forced his psyche to offer up the real problem. He wasn't getting any mileage or relief out of diffuse irritation. Her refusal to engage in a nonproblem left him swimming in his own swamp. Left there to stew, the real issue came forth.

As soon as he was talking about the real problem, Maureen came to him and was right with him. She hadn't built up any anger toward him that would cause her to withdraw, because she took such good care of herself. Since she had protected herself so well, she felt no barriers to an empathetic response.

If you take good care of yourself, you can be fully present when the other person shifts. "Boy, I've been taking my bad mood out on you. I'm sorry. Okay, let me see what's really going on."

"I'm here for you."

ANGER BOUNDARIES

Anger has been much maligned in our culture, due to the harm done by its destructive cousin, rage. But anger—like sorrow, joy, and fear—is a basic human feeling that in its pure, direct, boundaried expression can have positive impact. Furthermore, such expression can cleanse both the person carrying the issue and his or her relationship with the other person.

The suppression of anger can cause a lot of trouble, giving rise to virulent progeny such as malice, passive aggression, hostility, rage, sabotage, hate, blame, guilt, controlling behavior, shame, self-blame, and self-destruction. Passive aggression—hit and run rage subtly disguised as sweetness or concern—has the particular characteristic of causing harm without the initiator looking wrong.

As a rule, my clients have spent years suppressing anger. They've pushed it so far down that they don't even know they are angry. Most of their feelings come forth in the form of tears, sadness, or self-blame. But if anger is the true feeling, sadness or any other stand-in will never fix it.

True, direct, boundaried anger flares, then fades. It gets brighter, and then it is done.

In contrast, rage, hostility, malice, passive aggression, and hate tend to breed. Because the focus of each of these expressions is directed at some external target, the true feeling—anger or grief—ends up not being expressed.

This is why rage never gets used up. Rage begets rage. When a person gives way to rage, it feeds on itself and gets hotter and more destructive. Hate crimes escalate because rage becomes directed at the wrong event or wrong person. The original anger about the true cause gets lost.

If I'm really angry at my spouse, but instead I yell at my goldfish, nothing moves forward. When we take out anger on an innocent being, we haven't fixed anything.

Even if my cronies and I were to organize a society against goldfish, and get people to wear leather jackets with a bold slash across a leering goldfish, and picket pet stores with signs denouncing the slimy nature of the average fish, my rage would only increase. Goldfish would just be a patsy for some underlying righteous anger that I was not expressing appropriately.

A surefire way to tell the difference between anger and rage is that rage takes prisoners. Rage doesn't back off until the other person is hurt. Rage seeks to draw blood, or its emotional equivalent. It needs to cause damage before it starts evaporating. Allowed to escalate, rage can eventually kill.

Anger is different. Anger is an energy that flows from an *internal* place. It does not need a target. It does not seek to hurt others.

In order for anger to dissipate, we must feel our true feeling, express it accurately, and talk about the true event. If I say I'm angry because my sister is late, but I'm actually angry because I feel her pets are more important to her than I am, I won't feel relief, even if she apologizes and promises to be early next time.

Only the truth will shift a feeling. In addition, the truth is an opportunity to let someone else know us. Thus, it improves our chances of being treated better in the future.

If I'm mad that you took the last of the milk, but I say I'm mad because you didn't mail my letter, I'm not going to feel better. Plus, if you care enough about me to want to change, you'll be paying attention to getting my letters mailed while guzzling up all the milk. I'm bound to be angry again.

Expressing our true feeling about a true incident lightens and enlightens. All the energy tied up in keeping the anger contained is released. After we've been angry in a healthy way, we have more energy.

In addition, we enlighten ourselves and the person we're talking to. They get accurate information about something that matters to us, and they might change their behavior in response. (Even if they don't, just the act of talking about our concern will help.)

When we express anger in a direct, healthy, boundaried way, we learn something about ourselves. We get a new slant on an old problem; we access a memory that has been in the shadows; we may even discover a subtle way in which we set up the problem ourselves.

A thousand times I've heard clients say, "It won't do any good if I tell her I'm angry. She doesn't hear me. It won't make any difference."

It'll make a difference to you. *Changing the other person is not the primary reason for expressing anger.* The primary reason is that it's there, and it's the truth. Like any other feeling, expressing it lets you release it.

Anger has good boundaries when it is expressed with direct, clear, honest words about the true issue, with your focus on your own insides, rather than on the person who triggered the anger.

Here are some examples of clearly expressed anger:

"I am angry."

"I am angry that you took the last piece of bread without telling me. I was so disappointed when I went to make the turkey sandwich that I was looking forward to all week, and the bread was gone."

"I'm angry that you laughed when I told you something that matters to me."

"I am angry that you said you would do this and you haven't. I am angry, angry, angry."

"I am angry at the choices you made. I am angry that you let this simmer between us an extra two days instead of engaging emotionally and letting us take care of this."

"Grrr."

A *grrr* is neither self-parody nor rage, but simply an expression of anger without accusation, blame, or apology. Sometimes we have a physical need when angry to make an angry noise. Growling—expressing anger through sound—can sometimes release the energy of anger swiftly.

In expressing healthy anger, it's natural to work back and forth between the specific behaviors that led to the anger and the feeling itself.

The boundaries that keep anger healthy include the following:

- Let your listener set the physical distance between the two of you. If the other person needs to move apart from you in order to feel comfortable hearing your anger, don't make that another issue.

- Avoid "you" statements. Don't call the other person names. Don't demean, undermine, degrade, disparage, or put down the other individual. Use "I" statements: *I feel, I want, I hurt.*
- Avoid sarcasm. That edges you into indirect anger and shifts your focus to the other person.
- Never, ever hit, squeeze, pinch, shake, yank, punch, corner, physically or emotionally threaten, throw, slap, or beat the other person. This is rage. *If you do any of the above even once, get help.* Talk to a therapist or counselor as soon as you can.
- If you need to express your anger physically, that's fine, but use an inanimate object. To help the energy come out (and to help the other person stay calm), announce what you're about to do. "I've got to hit some pillows now." "I've got to punch the couch." "I'm going to scream at the top of my lungs for a couple of minutes." "I've got to walk around and shake my hands and yell." Even while doing this, keep looking inward at what's going on inside your own body.
- Protect children from being frightened by the working-out process. If children are in the house and they haven't been taught what happens with healthy anger, have your conversation where they can't hear you. If a baby is in the house, you can still have the conversation, but without raising your voices. (High volume is not essential to moving through anger.) Or get a baby-sitter and go someplace where you can be free to be loud.
- You are responsible for the feeling you have and your expression of it. You are also liable for any harm done if you go too far. It is never accurate to say, "You made me hit you."

- It's not easy to listen to someone who is powerfully angry. Don't expect to be heard perfectly.
- If the other person interrupts you, sidetracks you, misses the point, drags up unrelated events, or responds to the small stuff but misses your main message, say so. Ask them to return to listening.
- When you've completed expressing yourself and the other person has listened reasonably well, say a genuine thank you. If you've gone deep enough within yourself, you'll feel a shift inside, sometimes a rush of relief or energy. The other person's listening played an important part, so acknowledge that.

BOUNDARIES FOR LISTENING TO SOMEONE ELSE'S ANGER

- Listen respectfully as long as the expression of anger is direct, honest, and clean.
- If you start to feel scared or too close to the energy of the other person's anger, move back. If the room is too small, go to another one, or go outside, or stand in different rooms in such a way that you can see each other through the doorway. (Again, be careful to stay out of earshot of children unless they've been taught about anger.)
- Do not accept sarcasm or any comment that is demeaning, degrading, or undermining. Give a warning by holding up your hand like a stop sign. If the demeaning behavior doesn't stop, say, "I'm willing to listen later when you're able to talk in a healthy way. For now, I'm going to do something else." Then do it. Never listen to sarcasm and "you" statements for more than a few minutes.

- If you feel defensive, the best thing to say is, "I feel defensive." Changing the subject, using humor inappropriately, focusing on minutiae while ignoring the big picture, or dragging up some old fight are not likely to help.
- Listen as best you can, trying to remember that the other person is a human being with legitimate concerns. Listening to someone else does not invalidate your side or constitute agreement.
- If you really did whatever the other person is mad about, admit it and apologize.

OTHER ANGER BOUNDARIES

1. Deal with issues in a timely fashion. Don't put off working them out.

2. Do not vent your anger at Steve by badmouthing him to Susan, who knows both of you. Sooner or later, this snake will come back to bite you.

3. If the person you are angry with is dead or impossible to communicate with, you can still vent your anger. Express the whole enchilada to a trustworthy friend or a competent professional.

4. Good anger boundaries include:

- Speaking your feelings
- Focusing your attention on your insides, not on externals
- Physically expressing your anger by pacing, gesturing, or hitting inanimate objects, such as pillows
- Announcing your intentions before making a loud noise or beating on a couch or pillow

- Identifying the actual issue that triggered the anger
- "I" statements
- Letting the listener determine their physical distance from you
- Protecting the children in the house from fear

5. Good anger boundaries do *not* include:

- Disparaging, demeaning, or shaming the other person
- Indirect, passive-aggressive comments
- Rage
- Physically hurting the other person
- Threatening the other person
- Sarcasm
- "You" statements
- Scaring the children

By keeping anger within healthy limits and expressing it in a healthy fashion, you strengthen your own integrity, and protect the wholeness of your relationships as well.

Healthy anger is like a thunderstorm that cleanses the air and returns humidity to a comfortable level. It may flash and thunder, but it's always flowing from that central place, opening a fresh, easy comfort behind it.

Chapter 9

MAKING AMENDS

Error is not such a great sin as denial.

—IRENE ALLEN, *QUAKER SILENCE*

A responsible person doesn't leave messes for others to tidy. Likewise, a grown-up doesn't leave consequences for someone else to handle.

Sam was driving too fast on an icy road when he veered off the side and crashed through a stranger's picket fence. No one saw him, and he could have backed up his car and crept away, no one the wiser that he had been responsible.

But Sam was an honorable person. After he extricated his car, he wrote a note to the homeowner. That weekend he showed up with replacement slats and a hammer and repaired the fence.

Sam made appropriate amends. He made a mistake, and he carried the complete consequences of his mistake. He didn't stick the homeowner with the repair.

The boundary Sam crossed was a literal one. He repaired his neighbor's physical boundary. When we cross someone's

emotional or psychological boundary, we create consequences for the other person as well. By making amends, we
can contribute to repair of the boundary, reduce the consequences, promote healing, and help restore (or establish)
trust.

An apology is words. It at least acknowledges our error and
the effect it has had on another person. Amends are actions.
We actually do something to repair the problem that resulted
from our mistake.

Making amends is a way to get free of the burden of our
mistakes. When we make a mistake that impinges on another
person, amends repair three things—the harm to the other
person, the harm to our relationship with them, and the
harm to ourselves.

Sam didn't think twice about doing the right thing after he
plowed into that fence, but what he did saved himself and a
stranger from a loss of energy. If he had driven off without a
word, he would have changed himself inside. He would have
had to harden up a little to ignore that he had done some
harm to someone's property. (Whenever we need to keep
from knowing something about ourselves, it costs us in
health and energy. This is why amends are as important for
ourselves as they are for the other guy.)

The amends we make should fit the nature of the mistake. If
we make a boundary error, inadvertently trespassing on
something important to someone else through ignorance or
forgetfulness, correcting our error is all it takes:

Jana chattered away, not letting her sister get a word in
edgewise. Finally Ladi interrupted her. "Hey, Jana, I need to
talk to you about something, too."

Jana was already aware that she could violate time boundaries inadvertently, so she brought her side of the conversation to a close and said, "You go, girl. I'm all ears."

Shaian used her key to enter her sister's house while Cher was on vacation. This was not a violation, because the sisters had free access to each other's homes.

However, Shaian knew that Cher would not lend her any clothes, not even if she asked for permission. Thus, when Shaian borrowed Cher's favorite dress—a delicate aqua pastel—for a special date, she knew she was violating her sister's possession boundary.

That night, Shaian spilled tomato sauce on the dress. By the time she got around to treating it, the stain was set. She daubed it as well as she could, then hung it back in Cher's closet.

Cher was furious when she discovered it. She knew that Shaian was the only one who could have worn the dress. She called her. "Shaian, you ruined my favorite dress."

"I'm sorry."

"I can't believe you borrowed it after I told you I didn't want you wearing my clothes anymore—and my favorite one, too."

"I know. I shouldn't have, but Laran asked me to the company dance. I like him so much. And this was really important. I didn't have anything good enough. And I couldn't afford a new dress. Your things are so much nicer than mine."

"That's because I take care of them," Cher said tartly. "I don't care how important the date was to you, it still wasn't okay to expressly ignore the limit I set."

"I know. I shouldn't have. I'm sorry." Shaian spoke breezily, obviously unconcerned. "Well, see you next weekend."

"Hold on there. Not so fast. How are you going to fix this?"

"What do you mean?"

"You can't just brush me off and skip away as if you have no responsibility for this mistake," said Cher. "How are you going to make amends?"

"Make amends?"

"Right. You can't just leave this for me to handle. You caused the problem. You fix it."

"What do you want me to do?"

"You can take it to the dry cleaners and see if they can fix it."

"What if they can't?"

"Then you owe me the two hundred fifty dollars that I paid for that dress."

"I can't afford that."

"Then you better hope the dry cleaner can fix it. The sooner, the better."

"You drop it off," said Shaian. "I'll pay for it."

"No," replied Cher. "You screwed up. You make the effort."

"Oh, all right," said Shaian, annoyed. "Put it by the door and I'll pick it up on the way home from work."

"Thank you."

In a perfect world, people would automatically admit to their mistakes and voluntarily offer amends. (Actually, many mature and emotionally healthy people do just that.) However, some people keep quiet about their mistakes and hope that people won't care or notice. Others, when informed of their errors, think "I'm sorry" is enough.

A trite "I'm sorry" does nothing to repair the mistake. If the victim is still stuck having to deal with the consequences of the other person's mistake, then adequate amends have not been made.

Shaian deliberately ignored her sister's boundary, deciding that her need took precedence over respect for her sister. She continued to act with disregard when she did so little to care for the stain while it was fresh. Putting it back in the closet without admitting it and leaving it for her sister to find compounded her violation.

Cher was right to call her on it immediately. When Shaian offered a flat "I'm sorry," not even a heartfelt apology, Cher asked for amends. She didn't wait for Shaian to catch on. When Shaian pretended to know nothing about what to do, Cher told her.

HIERARCHY OF AMENDS

1. Fix the Mistake

Lilith asked Jessie to drop her Visa payment into the mailbox on his way out of the driveway. He laid it on a shelf of his closet when he switched sweaters, and then forgot about it. A week passed before he discovered his mistake. By that time, the payment deadline was imminent.

He took the letter directly to the post office and sent the payment Express Mail. Then he explained all this to Lilith, saying that if she got a late penalty, he would pay it.

2. Transfer the Consequences

Raven left for vacation and asked Jill to deposit her paycheck for her. Jill made the deposit late the following week. As a result, three of Raven's checks bounced and the bank rescinded her cash card privileges. It was an ambiguous situation: Raven could have been clearer; Jill could have acted more quickly.

Jill offered to split the overdraft penalties with Raven. She also went to the bank with Raven and explained to the manager that it was her error, not Raven's, that caused the overdraft.

Doing favors becomes a boundary issue when the person granting the favors has a pattern of either 1) not following through, or 2) messing up in a way that leaves the requester in a worse position than if they'd handled the task themselves.

We all need help at times. If we trust in help that doesn't materialize or that makes even more work for us, we lose confidence and ease with that person. We tighten our boundaries with a friend who isn't dependable, but a friend who fixes mistakes or otherwise makes amends lets us reset our boundaries to their previous level of trust.

By paying a portion of the penalties, Jill transferred part of the consequences to herself. In doing so, she let Raven know that when the fault isn't clear, she'll shoulder a share of the responsibility.

3. Reciprocal Payback

Anita was an hour late to pick up her sister, Pam, on the day they'd set aside to celebrate Pam's birthday. This cost Pam some of the joy of her day. While she waited, her enthusiasm dimmed and she felt unimportant to her sister.

Anita arrived in a flurry of excuses, using them to ward off potential anger or confrontation from Pam. Then she switched to an exaggerated eagerness in an effort to pump up Pam's clearly reduced energy.

They settled into Anita's car, but before she turned the key, Pam put her hand on her sister's arm. "Anita, I need to say something, or I might not have the great time I want to have today."

Anita turned toward her.

Pam continued, "I was so excited that you wanted to give me this day for my birthday, but the longer I waited, the less important I felt. Waiting took the gloss off the day for me. I want to get it back, but I'm feeling down."

Anita listened fully, then drew her sister into her arms. "I'm so sorry. I love you so much. I get overwhelmed with my life sometimes and just can't get everything done in time. But I don't want my frenzy to spread out over you, too. I want to make it up to you. I know—you waited an hour for me, so let's go an hour longer than we planned. We'll still get all the time we counted on. Would that work for you?"

"It would, but what are you giving up? If this makes you more overwhelmed, I won't feel good about it."

"In the first place, that's my problem. Besides, love, you know my frenzy is a created situation. If I had one day more each week than everybody else, I'd still be overcommitted. I want to do this, I want us to have our full experience. I love you very much."

Pam's amends completely made up for the violation of Pam's time and energy boundary. Each woman did her part in getting this to work out.

Pam could have forced herself through the day without telling the truth. Anita could have used excuses or other defensive comments to shut Pam up. In either case, both would have lost some of the bonding and fun the day had to offer.

Anita thought of a way to pay back the time she'd taken from Pam. This sort of reciprocal payback is a good way to fix a time, tidiness, or possession violation. If, because of our own choices, misplaced priorities, or poor judgment, we've squandered someone else's time, we can give time back. If we take ten minutes, we can do something that frees ten minutes for the other person.

AMENDING A SERIOUS VIOLATION

Making amends is more difficult when we have violated not just a boundary but a person. Abuse alters a person's future in a negative way, sometimes drastically. True amends attempt to give back that person's future. (This is why homicide is the most serious of crimes: it is not possible to amend it. The victim has lost his future. Nothing can be done to get that back.)

Sara had been molested by her father when she was a child. It was an open secret within the family. Everyone knew about it, but no one talked about it. When Sara grew up, she had an aversion to family gatherings, and to her father.

The entire family acted as if Sara had no basis for avoiding her father. They expected her to show up for family events, converse pleasantly with Dad, and endure his hugs as he said good-bye. Time after time she shied away from him, avoided conversation with him, or made excuses for not attending. Although he was the one who caused the harm, she ended up being the one on the outside.

Years later, he entered a twelve-step program and seriously pursued recovery. He came to the point of admitting to himself the great wrong he had done to his daughter. He called her and asked her to have lunch with him. As they walked to the restaurant, he stopped at an overlook and began talking.

He acknowledged that he'd molested her. He expressed his profound sorrow for betraying her as a father, and for all she'd had to handle because of his actions. He volunteered to pay for therapy for her and to go with her to a therapist. He said he was entirely willing for her to express her hurt, her anger, and anything else about the harm his actions had caused in her life.

With his first words, tears washed Sara's cheeks, and by the time he stopped talking, she was sobbing. She accepted all his offers. She went to therapy. Eventually she asked him to her sessions, where she gradually learned that she could express herself fully. He listened without excuses to everything she needed to say. Later, when it became evident that her eating disorder was a consequence of the violation, he paid for her to receive treatment.

He also talked to his wife and his sons, taking responsibility with them as well, urging them to see Sara differently. He removed the stigma of outcast from her.

COMPLETE AMENDS FOR VIOLATING ANOTHER PERSON

- Admit the error or violation.
- Express true regret for all harm done.
- Find (or create) a setting where both people are safe so that the victim can express feelings and issues related to the violation.
- If treatment or therapy could help restore the victim's well-being, offer as much financial and time support for it as possible.
- If necessary, restore the victim's place in the family.

RECEIVING AMENDS

Sara did a good job receiving her father's amends and therefore did not miss out on her own healing. In contrast, Evelyn was furious with her mother, Maddy, for the years of abandonment she'd suffered due to her mother's drinking. In her forties, Maddy got sober, got spiritual, and tried to patch things up with her adult daughter.

She tried to establish new routines with Evelyn, inviting her to holiday events, shopping trips, and special sightseeing weekends. Maddy tried on several occasions to talk about the past, to admit her mistakes. She offered to pay for therapy for Evelyn and to go with Evelyn to her sessions. She wanted with all her heart to repair the rift and make things right with her daughter. She wanted Evelyn to have a chance at a more fulfilling life.

Evelyn was angry. She was so angry, she even rejected the overtures that would have benefited her. Evelyn preferred being miserable so long as it prolonged her mother's punishment. Hurting herself, she knew, hurt her mother. She was so filled with anger that she was willing to sacrifice her own life to express it.

When we become adults, we become responsible for our own happiness. Regardless of the consequences we bear for someone else's violations, responsibility for healing transfers to our shoulders when we grow up.

By accepting her father's amends, Sara opened herself to great healing. In contrast, Evelyn blocked her own deliverance when she shut out her mother's efforts.

Evelyn is angry, rightly so, but acting it out instead of expressing it directly is itself a violation, and it keeps her and her relationship with her mother trapped like flies in amber.

As strange as it sounds, Maddy's best chance at helping Evelyn, now that her daughter is so vested in resisting improvement, is for Maddy to attend to her own life and happiness. There's a slim chance that if Evelyn's punishment stops working, Evelyn will see that she might as well do something to feel better.

HEALTHY BOUNDARIES FOR ACCEPTING AMENDS

- Allow the perpetrator to admit their wrongs.
- Find a place where you will both be safe. Express your anger directly, using healthy anger boundaries.
- If you sense that the other person is concerned mostly for themselves, rather than reversing the harm done to you, cut the session short.
- If either of you shows any sign of becoming dangerous or violent, stop and leave.
- If the other person offers to pay for appropriate treatment or to otherwise reverse the harm, seriously consider accepting the offer.

STATUTE OF LIMITATIONS

"Let it go, Maria. That happened twenty years ago."

What's the difference between carrying a grudge and knowing that a relationship has been perpetually altered by a violation?

Nothing heals as completely as telling the truth, expressing genuine remorse, feeling empathy for the injured person, and making complete amends. Unfortunately, not everyone is capable of all this. Some folks can offer partial restitution or some token of regret, but (for whatever reason) are unable to do more.

If someone has made a mistake and is genuinely trying to make up for it—for example, if they show through actions that they care, even if they're unable to talk about the violation—we gain by being flexible enough to let that count.

If the harm they did is great, then a token effort simply may not be good enough. But if their error didn't cause very serious consequences, perhaps we can let go of our feelings and open ourselves, bit by bit, to a partially restored relationship as we see other contributions that person can offer us. You are the only one who can judge whether someone's offering qualifies.

One final thought: have you done your part by letting the other person know that their action hurt you? Granted, some violations are obvious, but not everyone realizes when they've committed a garden-variety boundary violation. If they don't know, and you want amends made, you'll have to tell them.

For serious violations there is no statute of limitations. An amends twenty or thirty years after the injury can still bring great and lasting healing.

CALLING FOR AMENDS FROM THOSE WHO GOVERN

As a society, we Americans have endured victimization. Attorneys and lawmakers with their eyes on their careers have twisted good laws into pretzels. The legal system has seriously confused itself, using causes as excuses and even permission to continue abuse.

Today, three or more women must be raped before a rapist

loses his hunting privileges. Three or more people must die—or three or more children must be abducted—before a predator is removed from the community. What would happen to my livestock if I gave every predator three chances before I acted decisively?

Certain cultures in the world adamantly refuse to allow harm to come to their children. If we wanted to, we Americans could become just as powerful, without risking the spirit of the Constitution that we cherish deeply.

Any time a child's well-being is threatened, we must intervene—and do so powerfully, so that the child and future children can be saved from the potential acts of a predator. We must unite as a people to safeguard our children.

Nearly every way we are endangered by others is due to the harm those people received as children. Abusers were abused; rapists were raped. Powermongers were powerless. Woman-haters were taught to hate.

When children are irrevocably harmed, they can grow up to become predators and abusers. This is a good reason to put money into programs for children.

We *can* stop the cycle of abuse. We have the science to do it. Now we need the united will, the funding, and the laws to make it happen.

Chapter 10

FRIENDSHIP BOUNDARIES

Friendships fall on a continuum ranging from casual acquaintances to intimate soulmates. Behavior appropriate to one degree of friendship may not be appropriate with others.

DEGREES OF FRIENDSHIP

Acquaintances

Ranging from people you recognize to those you like a lot but don't know very well, an acquaintance is the first level of friendship. Although with some people you can jump to intimacy when you first lay eyes on each other, most of the time, deeper levels of friendship grow from having first been acquainted.

Neighbors

Even though we commonly use this term for someone who lives near us, it can also refer to someone with whom we share a similar situation. It is a step beyond mere acquaintanceship.

We can have a neighborly relationship with other church members; people with whom we share an interest, cause, or hobby; work companions; colleagues; and fellow travelers. Our lives overlap. We know them, might like them very much, and know something about them. Yet these are casual friends. Our contacts with them are low in intensity. An occasional event might increase our contact, but then when it's over we move back our usual distance.

If you are seeking deeper relationships, neighbors—geographical or situational—are good candidates because you have something in common.

Comrades

You know at least one aspect of a comrade well, and you like them very much. You normally share some activity or purpose, and spend regular time together doing it. Over time, a comrade may well become an intimate.

Your relationship spreads over a wider territory than with an acquaintance or neighbor. You learn how this person operates—their openness, moods, attitude, dependability, humor, integrity, their willingness to pitch in.

Intimates

An intimate friend, bosom buddy, soul mate, or crony is one of the great gifts of life. You can trust this person with your secrets, count on them when things are tough, and know that they are on your side. You know each other very well.

Once you've reached this level of friendship, you can move to opposite ends of the earth and yet connect fully in the blink of an eye. Each reciprocates when the other reaches out, and both grab the opportunities that are offered for being together.

Most intimate friends have similar values, shared interests, commonality of purpose, and like perspectives. They develop a history together that can, eventually, span decades. We can love intimate friends deeply.

CONTEXT

The degree and depth of your friendship defines its context. A request that would be completely appropriate toward a comrade or intimate might be out of line with an acquaintance or neighbor. Acting appropriately within the context of a particular friendship builds trust and can help it advance to a deeper level. Acting inappropriately prevents progress toward intimacy.

There can be exceptions according to the setting—you might experience great intimacy with a near stranger at a twelve-step recovery meeting, even though you know nothing about each other—but in ordinary circumstances, the degree of friendship sets the range for appropriate behavior.

Here's a breakdown of what's generally considered comfortable and appropriate behavior as it relates to the context of a friendship:

Use this chart not as a hard-and-fast rule but as a guideline. Your own insides are the best indicator of appropriate limits. If someone makes a request that seems presumptuous, say no. If someone hugs you and it doesn't feel right,

	Acquaintance	Neighbor	Comrade	Intimate
Give or get ride to airport	x	x	x	x
Help move	x	x	x	x
Call in middle of night because you have a great idea				x
Call in middle of night because you have an emergency		x	x	x
Tell deepest secret				x
Invite to Thanksgiving dinner	x	x	x	x
Hug spontaneously			x	x
Hold when crying			x	x
Invite yourself to their dinner			x	x
Stay overnight casually			x	x
Stay overnight for a special reason		x	x	x
Hang out with		x	x	x
Call frequently			x	x
Contact once a year	x	x		
Cuddle				x
Touch hands when sad	x	x	x	x
Hold hands				x
Talk about problems			x	x
Share worries		x	x	x
Chat about local events	x	x	x	x
Ask for a favor		x	x	x

that's all you need to know. Pull out of the hug immediately and say something like, "Please don't. I'm not comfortable with hugging yet."

Almost any of the actions on the chart could be appropriate in extraordinary circumstances. For example, waiting at a hospital for news of the results of a friend's surgery, you might spontaneously hug your friend's mother, whom you've only just met, when the surgeon gives you good news.

Different people have different styles, so just because it can be appropriate to cuddle with an intimate friend (who is not a spouse or lover) doesn't mean all intimate friends would be comfortable with it. Touch is always at the option of both people, and both should agree to it for it to happen.

Some people touch virtually everyone in friendliness and affection. Others tend to make very little physical contact. Both styles are normal, sane, and appropriate. As a rule, before touching or hugging a person for the first time, ask if it's okay.

Different regions and cultures also draw different lines for contact between casual and intimate friends. In certain conclaves of New England, even intimates don't hug. In California, intimacy with strangers is quickly established.

One caution, however. Quickly sprung intimacy isn't based on anything. You aren't known. You don't know the other person. You have no real idea how trustworthy the other person is. There is no true allegiance between you. So be careful about risking too much with a person who behaves intimately very quickly. See how they handle a small risk before you plunge deeper.

CIRCUMSTANCES

The current condition of your friendship also defines appropriate behavior. If you and Coupe are in the middle of a serious conflict, it's not a good time to ask him to run a frivolous errand. A request is jarring when it doesn't fit the current circumstances of the friendship. Put it on hold until matters are worked out.

Babe was friends with Marti and Gail, who originally did not know each other, but who met often at Babe's events. Later, Marti and Gail became neighbors. Marti liked Gail, even considered her a comrade, and began including her socially for her own sake, not just because she was Babe's friend.

Then one day Babe and Gail had a serious disagreement. They didn't work it out and stopped all contact with each other. When Marti attempted to talk to Gail, she got the cold shoulder herself.

Marti had had no contact from Gail for two years when she got this message: "Marti, this is Gail. I left my purse at Tam's house. Since she lives just a mile from you, would you pick up my purse and take it with you to your office? Just leave it with the receptionist and I'll get it from her."

What is your reaction to this request?

- It seems out of place. Something's missing.
- Too weird.
- What's the problem? Take her the purse.
- Seems appropriate.
- Maybe Gail's trying to reestablish the friendship.

Gail isn't using the purse as an excuse to reestablish the friendship. She doesn't even want to see Marti, and wants her to leave the purse with the receptionist so that they don't have to meet.

Under the circumstances, this request is surprising. The two people are no longer in a relationship. Gail was the one who broke off the friendship. For her to ask a favor, even a casual one, of Marti is inappropriate. Marti could reasonably ignore the message and do nothing. She owes Gail nothing.

Can you tell what is missing in Gail's request? See if you can sense it or figure it out—it will help you make sense of future communications that feel strange to you.

Gail didn't acknowledge the current state of her relationship with Marti. She ignored both the context and the circumstance.

The following message would be far more appropriate:

"Marti, this is Gail. I realize we haven't spoken in two years and that I'm the one who cut things off. I have a favor to ask, and ordinarily I wouldn't, but my situation is such that extra driving is hard for me. I left my purse at Tam's house. Would you be willing to pick it up and bring it to your office? I'm not trying to restart the friendship, and I know you don't owe me anything. I'd still appreciate it if you'd be willing to help me."

This statement acknowledges the current circumstances of the relationship. It does not attempt to manipulate. It doesn't hold out hope that this might be an opening into working things out. It states clearly that the request is outside the normal expectations for ex-friends.

When Gail made her original request without acknowledging the circumstances, she left it for Marti to do the work of processing an abnormal request and figuring out what to do about it.

Of course, if you are riding a bus that turns over, even your worst enemy deserves a hand. There's no time to acknowledge the situation. Afterward, though, it is gracious to do so. "Thanks for pulling me from the burning bus. I was rude to you three years ago, and you still helped me. I appreciate it."

RECIPROCITY

The distance to your house is the same as the distance to my house. A healthy relationship, regardless of the level of intimacy, is reciprocal. Give and take between two people match.

Char and Jenny became friends because their husbands worked together. Char was a quiet, perceptive person; Jenny was the type that sparkles. Char would invite a few people to casual dinners. Jenny would throw big parties.

Char gradually became Jenny's righthand woman before a party. She was dependable and efficient, and Jenny could count on her to quietly slice carrots or create an appetizer tray. They got so accustomed to the arrangement that before Jenny planned a party, she'd first make sure Char was available.

Char invited Jenny and her husband to events at her house as well. These were small and uncomplicated, and she didn't need much help, but, even so, Jenny neglected to offer any assistance. She stayed out of the kitchen and socialized with the men.

Then Jenny's husband got a big promotion and they moved to the swank part of town. Jenny could now afford to hire a caterer. Char continued to include Jenny and her husband at occasional dinners. But after the promotion, Jenny never invited Gail to a single event.

GIVING TOO MUCH

If you regularly give more to a relationship than the other person, something is off kilter. Perhaps the relationship means more to you or perhaps the other person is a taker.

Do you have a relationship in which you do most of the initiating? Are you the one who calls the other? Do you issue the invitations? Are you often in the role of helping the other person?

You can talk to your friend about this pattern, or you can reduce or eliminate your contact with them for a while and see what happens. Sometimes, the other person will realize you are missing and begin to take up the slack. But sometimes the pattern is so firmly established that it'll take some real effort on both your parts to restore balance.

TAKING TOO MUCH

Are you in a relationship where you let the other person do most or all of the work? Do you let the other guy carry the job of keeping the relationship going? Do you get absorbed with what you are doing and forget about the other person's needs?

One way to tell that you may be taking too much is if you have revolving-door relationships. Do you have a new set of friends every two years? Then it's possible that as your buddies catch on to your lack of involvement, they move on.

If you want to discover the joys of true friendship, return favors. Give back. Plan and invite your friend to an event they'd enjoy. Initiate a phone call, even if you feel nervous at first. You may discover that one of the true pleasures of life is to please or surprise a friend.

THEY WANT MORE. YOU DON'T.

What if you feel that you are, at most, a comrade to another person, and yet they behave as though you were intimates? Set a boundary. Once a relationship has gone as far as you want it to, say so. Clearly express or demonstrate your limits. Continue to enjoy being on the same bowling team, but don't issue or respond to invitations to more personal family get-togethers.

WHEN YOU WANT MORE

Perhaps you'd like to progress to the next level of intimacy with someone, but you're not sure they're interested. What should you do? Issue an invitation or take some small risks, and see how it goes.

If you keep getting turned down, you can either stop asking, or talk to the person about it to clarify the situation (unless their refusals have been unequivocal).

"Say, Edgar, I've been inviting you to join us on the fishing boat because I'd like to know you better."

"Me too, Sam. I just don't like fish. That's why I keep turning you down."

"Like fried rattlesnake?"

"My favorite."

"Want to come to my house for a rattlesnake feast?"

"Love to."

My personal number for effort is three. If I make three calls, issue three invitations, or take three risks, and the other person hasn't said yes or reciprocated, I stop. Three strikes and I quit trying. It's up to you to decide your own limit. A reasonable range is between two and five.

If you are open to a closer relationship with someone but need to refuse their invitation, be sure to say that they are not the reason for your thumbs-down. Make a counterinvitation at some point to reinforce that message.

Once you turn someone down three times in a row, the ball's definitely in your court. It's your turn to make an effort.

Also pay attention when a friend demonstrates a different value system from your own. If your friend borrows things and doesn't return them, or is not always truthful, or is hot one day and cold the next, be careful about advancing the relationship. You deserve friends who are consistent, considerate, and thoughtful. Back out of any relationship in which you are repeatedly treated with disregard.

WHEN FRIENDS MAKE MISTAKES

We don't always realize when we've screwed up with a friend, because they usually cut us a lot of slack. A person making an honest mistake is different from one with Swiss cheese values, so as you build history together, you will soon be able to observe which is the case.

As hard as it can be, telling the truth when a friend makes a mistake can actually catapult both of you to a *higher* level of trust. A little formula that works well when you need to express something difficult is, "When you_____, I felt_____."

"When you didn't return my call, I felt forgotten."

"When you were twenty minutes late to the movie, I was angry. I want you to be on time. I hate waiting and worrying about you, and feeling like I'm at the bottom of your list."

A lack of honest communication has killed many a budding friendship. When people clam up and don't explain that they've been hurt, the other person has no way of knowing what went wrong. It may seem obvious to you, but the other guy may not know their exact mistake—or that they've made a mistake at all—unless you tell them.

They may even pick up on your anger and try to make amends, but without your specific information, they could try to improve the wrong thing.

KEEPING CONFIDENCES

Perhaps the most important friendship boundary is this one: don't gossip about a friend to another person.

Don't pass on negative information, and don't reveal what they've told you in confidence. It takes discipline to protect private information, but it's worth the payoff in being trusted.

When I was in college I shared a minuscule apartment with three other women. We all slept in bunk beds in a tiny bed room. One night, two of my roommates came back early and thought I was still on a date. They began talking about me, not knowing I had gone to bed early on my top bunk. I listened to them putting me down. After a while, I got up, dressed, and to their surprise, appeared in the living room. I said nothing to them, just walked out of the apartment and downstairs to express my hurt to friends I trusted. The incident squashed my relationship with those two women.

FRIENDSHIP BOUNDARIES

Certain boundaries protect the integrity of friendship. These include a recognition of the context of the relationship, awareness of the current circumstances between you and the other person, reciprocity, parity, trustworthiness, communication, and confidentiality. Keep good boundaries with friends and your friendships will have the safety that will enable them to grow.

Chapter 11

GOSSIP GOSSIP GOSSIP
(OR TRIANGULATION)

"Anastasia, this is Branwen. You should have seen what Cas wore to the party. It was appalling."

Gossip is talking about someone who is not present, usually in a negative way. It is a form of triangulation.

Triangulation occurs when three points are created by an interaction that sets one person outside the conversation or connection between two other people. When Branwen talks negatively to Anastasia about Cas, Anastasia and Branwen are drawn together by making Cas an outsider. Cas is the target, the one being triangulated.

Through triangulation you can create an issue between the target and the person you're talking to without their even knowing this is happening. "Branwen, I saw Cas sucking up to the boss. I hope she doesn't finagle the assignment you want." Branwen now has a reason to be wary about Cas. Anastasia has fostered competition between Branwen and Cas where none may have existed.

Gossip can also be used to discharge feelings. "Anastasia, I

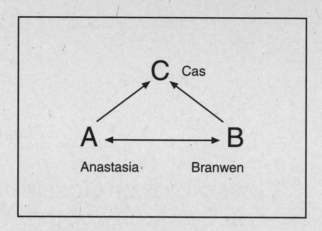

am *so* mad at Jolie. She got assigned the desk next to the window. I wanted that desk. I wonder what she did to make the boss cough it up for her."

What are the potential consequences of this communication?

- Branwen gets rid of her anger toward Jolie.
- Anastasia may now have negative feelings toward Jolie.
- Jolie may be unaware that Branwen and Anastasia have teamed up, leaving her on the outside.
- Anastasia learns that Branwen doesn't handle issues directly and that she too may be the subject of gossip if Branwen becomes unhappy with her.

Any of the above consequences could result from Branwen's triangulation or gossip. One thing is certain: if Branwen continues to handle problems this way, she won't get what she wants. As hard as it may be for her to be direct, Branwen's best chance of getting a desk by the window is to talk to the boss about it directly.

PROBLEMS WITH GOSSIP

Gossip doesn't get things done. It may sow discord and unease, but it doesn't fix problems or improve situations. It is a violation of healthy communication boundaries.

Gossip doesn't heal feelings. Branwen is venting to Anastasia, but will this fix her issue with Jolie? No. She'll still be irritated with Jolie. Gossip may vent the immediate steam, but the conflict with the original person still remains.

Gossip puts people on the alert. Most of us figure that if you gossip to me about her, you'll gossip to her about me. (And we're usually right.)

Gossip fragments the community. It causes people to take sides unnecessarily and can create distance between people who may not actually have an issue with each other.

Gossip does not—and cannot—create intimacy. Although Cas is made an outsider when Branwen and Anastasia gossip about her, Branwen and Anastasia aren't actually improving their relationship. Their eyes are on Cas, not on each other. They aren't building any true connection with each other.

GOSSIP VERSUS CLARIFICATION

What is the difference between gossiping and getting clarification from someone? Kimiko and Magda meet every week for lunch. Words fly fast as they talk in vivid detail about their husbands. Is this gossip? No, it's a clarifying process.

The purpose of gossip is to draw the listener to your side and away from the absent person. Magda isn't trying to pit Kimiko against Ron; she just wants to figure out where she got lost in her argument with him. The point of her detailed play-by-play is for Magda to understand more about how to help herself in her intimate relationship.

Two hallmarks distinguish gossip from a clarifying discussion. First, with gossip, the absent person is equidistant to the two talkers. In a clarifying discussion, the absent person is generally closer to the talker than to the listener.

When I tell you about the outrageous thing my mother did, it's *my* mother. She's closer to me than she is to you. I'm not trying to pull you to my side. You're probably already on my side.

The second difference is that a clarifying conversation leads to action on the part of the speaker. The outcome of this autopsy of my fight with my mother will be that I will say something to her or that I will take better care of myself.

The outcome of gossip is that the *listener* is stimulated to action, even if the action is nothing more than a slight withdrawal from the absent person.

Two friends who have a clarifying discussion about a third friend must share it with her afterward if all three people are to maintain healthy connection. If the conversation is not taken back to the absent person, it is gossip.

Let's say Amanita, Sonja, and Amber are all good friends. Amanita is miffed at Sonja and talks about it to Amber. To maintain health among all three friends, the next conversation should include Sonja, revealing both that Amanita was miffed and that she talked to Amber about it.

If these things aren't said, Amanita and Amber will be holding a secret against Sonja. The energy will shift in the relationships and Sonja will be removed a pace from the other two. All will be affected by this, even though Sonja has no conscious knowledge about what happened.

THE TOWN CRIER

When secrets take root, a community can become unhealthy with amazing speed. Now and then an office or community will be afflicted with someone who purposely sows discord among the population, primarily to enhance their own position. A slighting comment here, an almost imperceptible slam there, and members draw back from one another. I've seen this so skillfully done that no one realizes they have been pitted against the others.

Some signs that a town crier is at work in your environment include:

- Feeling alienated from others
- Having anger toward someone even though that person has done nothing directly to you
- Feeling mistrustful of others even though they've done nothing to lose your trust
- Having intimate information about someone that that person did not tell you

If you sense that you are being manipulated to think badly of someone, there's an easy way to fix the situation: deliberately speak to the person you're starting to dislike. Discuss this issue with them. Find out for yourself if the information you've been given jibes with reality.

What if you suspect that *you've* been the target of gossip? Check with people to see if they have been handed negative information about you. Invite them to be honest and to give you a chance to correct misinformation they may have been given. When enough of you unite to expose the pattern, you will render the town crier impotent. You can also confront them about their behavior and tell them to stop.

In an office or business, an alert supervisor will notice if discord or trouble occurs most frequently in the vicinity of a certain person. Even if that person always appears innocent and other people seem always at fault, investigation into the matter is called for. A boss may have to call people in one by one in order to trace the origin of the problem.

Unfortunately, if the boss is the one giving different stories to everyone, the staff will be forced to gossip to find out what's really going on. I have witnessed many situations where a business owner sabotaged the success of his own company by being secretive, by favoring some employees over others, by giving different stories to different people, and by gossiping about certain employees to other employees. These business owners didn't seem to realize that creating alienation among staff members reduced cooperation and goodwill.

A boss who doesn't follow clean communication principles will foster a workforce of snipers. Employee energy will be used for self-protection rather than productive work. People will keep good ideas to themselves and be more concerned with personal advancement or security than with the mission of the organization. They will be more likely to form cliques, so that they have safe alignment somewhere within the ranks. They will waste time gossiping, either to undermine others or to scope out what's really happening in the company.

In a neighborhood, church, office, or in friendships, avoiding gossip increases the health of the community. Since gossip deflects feeling without handling issues, refusing to gossip forces us to face issues directly with the people involved.

I'm impressed that in my own circles—in my neighborhood, friendships, and community—no one gossips. If a comment is made about someone not present, it is either positive or informational. "She's gone for a week to visit her kids." Or, "He's a great gardener."

We are responsible for being careful when we find that we are talking to someone who is not using healthy communication skills. If that person is attempting to manipulate, control, or harm us (or others), then we need to limit what we reveal to them.

Research has shown that a listener's first response to a gossiper determines the course of the conversation. Contrast how each of the following responses would affect you if you were trying to start a gossip fest:

Situation 1

You: "Amy looks like she tied one on last night."
Listener: "You should have seen her at the party Friday."

Situation 2

You: "Amy looks like she tied one on last night."
Listener: "I hope nothing's wrong. I'm going to ask her how she's doing."

You have the power to halt gossip in its tracks by a response that says, "I won't join with you in disparaging someone else." You can also be direct: "Amala, I find that I feel better when I look for the positive traits in a person. Please don't share thoughts like that with me."

Communication is best used to direct, inform, and empower. The purest purpose of communication is to increase understanding on all sides. When healthy communication skills are used, the integrity of a relationship is strengthened.

Chapter 12

INTIMACY BOUNDARIES

Intimacy is *the* challenge of life. As I sail steadfastly into the deepening seas of my fifties and leave a longer wake behind me, I see that nothing is more important than one's relationship with self and others—not career, not keeping the house perfect, not amassing possessions. Learning to love, to be genuine, and to gracefully allow others entrance into our hearts—these are the profound challenges for which we were born.

For some of us, the challenge is greater than for others. If we were born into hate, need, sickness, selfishness, addiction, or callousness, we learned survival skills antithetical to those used for developing intimacy.

Just as we are eventually invited to make the transition from surviving to living, we are similarly beckoned from isolation into intimacy. The invitation may come from a wife, husband, lover, or friend.

Intimacy absolutely requires that each person in a relationship be whole and individual. Codependence is not intimacy. Enmeshment—two people blending in such a way that one or both lose their identity—is not intimacy either.

Intimacy comes when two people, both standing clearly in their own lives—with their faults and their truths, their needs and their gifts—say to each other, "This is me. I see you. I am willing to say the whole truth, make mistakes, forgive, trust, receive, give, allow our differences, argue, laugh, and stand together with you in awe."

Not all intimates are lovers. Not all lovers are intimates. A friendship can achieve great intimacy and be entirely nonsexual.

Not all intimates are married to each other. Not all spouses are intimates. Marriage is a tremendous opportunity for intimacy, but many spouses miss the point.

The growth of intimacy will teach us how to love—both ourselves and the other person. If we will allow ourselves to practice the skills of intimacy, we will learn to love.

Boundaries protect love and intimacy. Certain behaviors support the integrity of intimacy. Other behaviors harm, disrupt, or reverse intimacy. By using the skills that promote intimacy, boundaries are created that protect the relationship.

In every one of your relationships, you are on a continuum between intimacy and separation. You stand on a slide that tilts you toward either intimacy or separateness. Exactly where you stand at any given moment is the result of your decisions, your feelings, how you handle situations, and the way you and the other person communicate.

Think of any friend. Your relationship with each other is fluid. It is constantly shifting either closer or further apart, depending on what each of you does.

If you are both making decisions that promote intimacy, you become steadily closer and the boundaries strengthen. If one or both of you acts against intimacy, however, you move toward separation. It is hard for only one person to keep intimacy going if the other is acting against intimacy.

• • •

Amalia and Esther were friends who liked to travel together. On a vacation in Florida, at the end of a lazy day of swimming and sunbathing, they were equally relaxed and sun-logged. Esther was showering at a beachside changing room and realized she'd left her undies in the trunk of the car. Amalia was dressed. With a light spirit, Amalia offered to go to the car for Esther. She walked the humid streets three blocks to where the car was parked, found Esther's undies, and brought them back to the shower room. "Here they are!" Amalia sang.

Esther responded, "Did you bring my bra?"

Amalia answered, "No, I didn't realize you needed it."

Esther said grumpily, "Well, why wouldn't I?"

Esther's response shifted this relationship toward separation. How big a shift would depend on whether she does this kind of thing a lot, and whether she realizes what she's doing and can make a compensating action toward intimacy.

We all make mistakes with intimacy. What is right for us may be hard on the relationship, or vice versa. We all have moments of thoughtlessness and self-absorption. However, we *invite* separation when we are so focused on ourselves that we expect others to anticipate our needs, or when we take their benevolence for granted. A healthy person moves between awareness of self and awareness of relationship.

INTIMACY SKILLS

- Noticing when others extend themselves for you
- Appreciating gifts of time, effort, money, energy, attention, and thoughtfulness
- Taking responsibility for communicating your needs

Meerkurk and Julia Penn were on their honeymoon. Although they had dated for a couple of years and lived back and forth in each other's apartments, they had never been together nonstop in the same space for more than a week at a time. Now, in the third week of their marriage, Meerkurk had gotten quieter and quieter.

As they both gazed down at the mountain-framed turquoise waters of Diablo Lake, a scene of peace and great beauty, Julia tried to nestle into Meerkurk's arms. He stiffened. She pulled back, hurt.

Trying for connection, she said, "This is so incredible. Look at the sun's rays bouncing off that glacier." Meerkurk was silent, not even looking where she pointed.

She moved a little apart, wondering what she had done. Silently, they got into the car and drove on.

Clearly, Meerkurk's unresponsiveness shifted their relationship toward separation. They were having a problem many newly joined couples experience: they weren't having enough time alone and apart.

Meerkurk was pushing Julia away. In the short run, this method usually nets the opposite of what is desired. When you pull away from someone who's been close, they are likely first to move toward you rather than away from you. So Meerkurk, by withdrawing, got the opposite of what he needed. Over time, such withdrawing and nonresponsiveness would create a gulf in the relationship, and he would lose her full presence even when he wanted it.

As two people blend their lives, it is still important for them to nourish themselves as individuals. This may mean time together but not interacting (such as reading or going to a movie), time separate, and time with others. Someone who is used to living alone will continue to need periods of quiet, of reflection and restoration. When people begin living together, individual pursuits must still be arranged.

What might Meerkurk have done differently? He could say something like this: "Hon, I just realized I need some alone time. I'm just not taking this in, because I'm kind of full up. I can think of some options. We can go back to the inn and you can read or sit in the sun while I go on a hike, or I could sit here awhile and you could take the car to Newhalem and walk through the forestry exhibit you were interested in."

A boundary always protects the integrity of something. Meerkurk (in this healthier replay of the situation) created a boundary when he honestly expressed his need for solitude. He also protected the integrity of the marriage by stating that need directly and in a way that was considerate of Julia.

Good boundaries, created by the use of good intimacy skills, keep a committed or intimate relationship lightly balanced between the needs of the individual and the needs of the relationship.

INTIMACY SKILLS

- State your needs directly.
- Be honest about your feelings.
- Acknowledge your true, current position in the relationship, even though it may be hard for the other person to hear.
- Connect any shift toward separation with the events that caused it.
- Say what will restore you and make you available again for intimacy.

THE DOUGHNUT DEFINES THE DOUGHNUT HOLE

One of the most difficult concepts to grasp about boundaries is that they also define what should be *present* in a relationship. For example, a committed relationship includes attention from each person to the other. *The absence of attention is a boundary violation.* (Remember that a boundary protects the integrity of something. Shared experience protects the integrity of a relationship.)

If you and your mate are too often and too long apart, or if you don't have regular moments of focusing on each other, you are violating the boundary of closeness. The integrity of the relationship can be threatened if the two of you live so separately as to be virtual strangers, neither of you in touch with the blood and passions and terrors of the other. Having regular focused time together creates a boundary that protects the integrity of your connection.

The boundaries of intimacy are injured when a mate refuses to work out an issue, rejects the other person's efforts to make amends, remains coldly aloof, or stays emotionally unavailable. These are all actions that create separation.

INTIMACY BOUNDARIES VERSUS PERSONAL BOUNDARIES

Intimacy boundaries do not require us to violate our own personal boundaries. Yet we violate our own boundaries, and ourselves, when we act against our own internal guidance in order to ostensibly "protect" our relationship with someone else.

If we force ourselves to stand near a healthy spouse with poor hygiene whose body odor repels us, we diminish ourselves. If we force ourselves to be closer to an angry person than feels safe to us, we send a shock through our system. If we make ourselves endure an embrace from someone who has harmed us and who has not made adequate amends, we violate ourselves. If we endure an unwanted sexual act in order to placate or hang on to someone else, we rip our spirits.

We are responsible for taking ourselves out of situations that demean us and for avoiding people who malign us. If we don't, we violate our own boundaries. We diminish our own integrity by not holding to the limits that would keep us from being exploited, demeaned, or treated with disregard.

What relationship do you think you are protecting if you let someone else belittle you? What family unit are you preserving if all your relatives allow one member to scapegoat another?

Even if you can't explain it or make a good case for it, if you get a strong internal message to move away from a person or a situation, you do yourself right by honoring it. Then, at a distance, you can talk to someone about it or think out what's going on.

Anya, Joan, and Mahla have been friends since college. They were on the varsity basketball team together, and now, in midlife, they get together for a reunion at the NBA playoffs each year. They meet in the city of the contest, get a swank room at an expensive hotel, shop, eat at fancy restaurants, and watch the games. Each year, easy camaraderie spreads among them immediately. They tease each other, laugh, and catch up on each other's lives.

But at their eleventh such get-together they faced a surprising new situation. Mahla seemed to talk a lot, cutting in when another person was talking, and she never apologized or asked the other person to resume her conversation. She got agitated when they were seated fifteen minutes late for their dinner reservation. She was outraged when she was served fries instead of a baked potato. She paced restlessly when they couldn't find a cab.

Anya and Joan thought something must be wrong for Mahla at home and tried various questions to draw her out. But each time, Mahla either changed the subject or didn't answer at all.

Here are some of Anya and Joan's options:

1. Endure the rest of the week, and find some excuse for not meeting next year
2. Withdraw from Mahla and spend more time with each other
3. Confront Mahla and talk about how her behavior is affecting them

The first two options are drifts toward separation. Only option 3 offers the possibility of moving the three women toward intimacy.

We all make mistakes. We inadvertently hurt a friend's feelings, or miss an important cue, or say something unwittingly unkind. We let too much time pass before calling. We miss a birthday. We buy someone pickles when they told us years ago that pickles remind them of their mean old aunt.

Sooner or later, any thriving relationship will run into a situation where someone screws up without realizing it. If you're the one who gets hurt or forgotten, you have to say so to the person who hurt you. If you keep mum, you'll lose energy and trust for the relationship. You'll also risk being treated the same way again.

So a most important part of intimacy boundaries involves confrontation. For example:

"Mahla, you seem frantic and wired this year. I'm worried

about you. Is something going on in your life that is making it hard for you to be here?"

Or "Mahla, you're acting so different this year. It's hurting our time together. Can we please talk about it?"

Buck called George at 6 A.M. "I know you asked me not to call this early, but I was trying to fix that furnace and I just can't get it going."

"Buck, this makes me mad. I've told you over and over not to call me before ten. I didn't get home from work till after midnight. I'm tired."

"I know, I know. But we're freezing over here. Would you please come over and help me out? My wife is coming down with a cold."

George has a different problem. Buck keeps disregarding George's limits. This is a situation where, to take care of himself, George will have to pull out of at least part of the relationship. He and Buck can still go fishing together, but they aren't really buddies. A true buddy doesn't ignore a friend's reasonable requests.

"Buck, don't call me again before ten. I'm hanging up. Good-bye."

George does not have to figure out Buck's furnace problem before taking care of himself. He does not have to make things okay for Buck first. He gets to pay attention to his body's tiredness, hang up, and go back to bed.

Intimacy Skills

- Respect limits set by the other person.
- Respect reasonable requests.

- Confront the other person when something they do (or fail to do) is beginning to have negative impact on your relationship.
- When the other person's action (or failure to act) feels disrespectful, thoughtless, or uncomfortable, say so.

SPOUSES, MATES, AND PARTNERS

When we look into another person's eyes and make a commitment to join our lives together, we launch an intention that is itself a boundary. We create a boundary when we give our word. Then we keep the boundary by what we do.

Whether such a pledge is sealed in a sanctuary before witnesses or is made privately on a mountaintop, boundaries make possible fulfillment of that commitment. Boundaries usher commitments into reality. Limits about what will be included and what will be excluded create intimacy.

BOUNDARIES THAT PROMOTE INTIMACY

- Express issues in a timely fashion.
- Speak as honestly as possible.
- Express your feelings in a healthy way.
- Make time for communication.
- Appreciate the other person's special efforts on your behalf.
- Soak up the other person's expressions of love. (For example, pause a moment when someone says, "I love you." Deliberately receive the meaning behind the words before responding.)

- Make regular times to enjoy leisure together.
- Share physical closeness that doesn't always lead to sex.
- Chat about the thoughts and events of your day. Give the other person a picture of the part of your day you spent separately. Listen fully as your partner does the same for you.
- Pay attention to other boundaries described in this book.
- Maintain sexual fidelity.
- When you realize you are heading toward an unexpected change, talk about it with your partner.
- Make important decisions together. Negotiate as necessary.
- Make amends when your partner has suffered negative consequences as a result of something you've done.
- When your partner does something that improves your life, respond with something that gives them joy.

In a marriage or life partnership, not using the skills of intimacy can be a boundary violation. For example, since open, nonthreatening communication is essential to the growth of any close relationship, the absence of it is a boundary violation. If something that is supposed to be part of the relationship is excluded, the integrity and the wholeness of the relationship are threatened.

VIOLATIONS OF INTIMACY BOUNDARIES

- Refusing to discuss important matters
- Making a decision that affects the other person's life without discussing it with them
- Staying physically separate

- Gratifying yourself sexually without consideration of the other's sexual needs or limits
- Sexual infidelity
- Treating the other person coldly or angrily rather than handling conflict directly
- Rage
- Refusing to acknowledge how you may have hurt the other person
- Not making amends for your mistakes

INTIMACY DERAILED

If you are in a relationship that is off track, boundaries can help to pull it back onto a course toward intimacy. Your relationship with your partner will improve if you both strive to keep within the boundaries described here—not only the boundaries that promote intimacy, but the ones that prevent apartness. Indeed, a great many mistakes can be corrected with the application of boundaries.

Nevertheless, sometimes a couple finds it hard to reverse the momentum toward separation. Sometimes their issues are piled as high as Mt. Everest, or their harmful practices have become a habit. A skilled therapist can create a path through the clutter.

What else can be done if a relationship has gotten close to separation? Here's a secret that comes to us from infant research. Studies have shown that a newborn may not start life as a cute baby. It's the act of touching a baby that causes it to become appealing.

We become drawn to a person when we take care of them. It's not just that we change by tending to someone. The other person also changes and becomes more attractive. We can feel a spark of affection grow when we act lovingly toward someone else.

Try the following: both of you make a spoken and honest commitment to act lovingly toward each other for exactly one month. Then, at the end of that month, reexamine your feelings and the relationship. See how attractive your mate becomes as a result of your warm attention.

Chapter 13

Holiday, Birthday, and Celebration Boundaries

Holidays and Vacations

We need holidays and celebrations. We need breaks from making a living so that we can enjoy living. However, one person's love is another person's labor; thus, what restores one person can be draining for someone else.

Your idea of a holiday may be basking on a beach yet you are married to a museum monger. You like Christmas with relatives to the rafters, but your spouse wants to go to the Sheraton for the buffet. You want a Valentine's Day with romantic dinner, soft music, five solid minutes of being adored, close dancing, and a roll in the hay. He'd prefer to toss you a card and get to the hay as quickly as possible.

What's a person to do? Lots of things: negotiate, compromise, and take turns.

Holidays and celebrations can strengthen relationships. We are drawn to people we can laugh and play with, so working out the bugs around holidays will give the relationship energy.

How is this a boundary issue? Our own needs for a holiday are important. Fruitful recreational time centers and strengthens us. On the other hand, a sabotaged vacation takes more out of us than if we hadn't gone away at all. We must be capable of protecting our recreational time or we'll pay the cost in illness or exhaustion.

Lisa loved Christmas. She was energized by every aspect—the music, decorations, spirit of giving, the smell of evergreens, the shopping. She married Sean, a man whose childhood household had disintegrated every Christmas. His father would be drunk by midmorning, his mother would grovel, and the kids would either cower from Dad or be wildly out of control.

Sean wanted to cancel Christmas. Since Lisa wouldn't consider such a thing, he subtly sabotaged each holiday instead. He was gruff in receiving her gifts. He'd get her one expensive present that was the wrong size or color. He'd rebuff her attempts to include him in her joy, and in so doing, chase her joy away. He was curt and impatient with guests, who soon felt uncomfortable and lost their spontaneity.

Lisa confronted Sean as their third Christmas approached. "Sean, let's talk about Christmas. I'm not going to go through another one like the last two."

"What do you mean?" He truly didn't know.

"You spend the day with a black cloud over your head, and you seem to want us to join you under it. Christmas is my favorite holiday. I want to see if we can work out a way to improve it for you and preserve it for me."

"I just want to cancel the whole thing," he said gruffly.

"I could tell, from your attitude last year. I didn't do anything to deserve the anger you were tossing around."

"I hate Christmas!"

"Are you willing to deal with your hate and anger about it?"

"What do you mean?"

"I love Christmas. If all you can do is spoil it, I want you to think of something else you'd like to do that day and go do it. I'd rather you be here, because I love you and I want you to be a part of it, but if that's more than you can do, then I want my day."

He was quiet. "What do you mean, deal with my anger?"

"I imagine, knowing what your parents were like, that Christmas was awful when you were a kid."

"You got that right. The old man made it open season on the innocents. My mom got thrown across the kitchen once because she put pepper in the gravy."

"No wonder you hate it. You must have gotten scared when Christmas was getting near."

"All the other kids were wild to get out of school, and afterward they'd talk about all their presents. I just wanted school to keep on going. We always had to write some dumb essay about 'My Favorite Christmas Gift' or some such. I never could think of anything to write."

"It was miserable."

"Yeah."

"I'm sorry it was like that."

"Yeah."

"Thanks for not drinking. I'm so glad you don't put us through that."

He looked surprised. "I swore I'd never touch a drop and I haven't. I wasn't going to end up the way the old man did."

"I know. I'm so glad you don't. But your attitude does spoil the holiday for me. I'm not scared or hurt by it the way you and your mother were, but I really like Christmas. Maybe you could let me show you how it could be fun."

"Maybe."

"Would you be willing to talk to Father Pat about it and let him help you with your memories?"

"What's happened, happened. Can't change the past."

"No, but we can change how it affects us. We can change how we feel about things."

"Okay. Will you go with me?"

"Sure."

This shows what can happen when you set a boundary and stay open to the way a conversation unfolds (and when you aren't met with defensiveness). We can be so strict in setting a boundary that we may miss that the thing we really want from it is starting to show up. Remember, the point in setting a boundary is to preserve something that matters. When you set a boundary and the other person starts to reveal something in a nondefensive manner, not to distract or derail you but to meet your issue in their own unique way, try to go with it.

Lisa stayed alert and kept her mind on her issue. She was able to recognize an approximation of negotiation. Sean was not a verbal man, not someone accustomed to identifying and working with his feelings. She helped him do something difficult. This led to new understanding and a shift in the problem, and it restored integrity to their relationship.

Some of us have good relationship skills, what I call a high relationship IQ. We can naturally see and do the things that grease the skids of a relationship. Other people, however—even other good people—may be more or less blind to the workings of relationship.

If you are fortunate enough to have a high relationship IQ, you will be blessed with good friends, but not all of them will be able to appreciate your contribution to the relationship. Sometimes that can be irritating; at other times though, you can see that you are compensated by the different gifts the other person offers you.

Lisa loved Sean, and she felt blessed by his goodness and his responsiveness when she needed any sort of gadget created in the household. She knew other husbands might take five years to fix a faucet, but when she slipped on the landing to the garage, Sean installed a nonskid surface and a handrail before the day was out—without her even asking him to do anything.

When we are facile at relationship skills we might insist that the other meet us at our same level of skill. Had Lisa done that, however, she'd have missed a great opportunity for strengthening their relationship. Had she insisted that he follow the purest communication rules—stick to the subject, hear her first, talk about his feelings—she would have lost his involvement. Such expectations would have been beyond him.

Purists might call Lisa codependent, but I call her generous and practical. She did not make the mistake of being controlling around the process of communication, and therefore they both took a step toward creating a holiday that would give them joy and bring them closer together.

HOW TO CREATE SUCCESSFUL HOLIDAYS

BEFORE THE HOLIDAY

- Talk about the holiday in advance. Each person take a turn describing how they'd like the holiday to be. Talk about activities, food, timing, costs, whom to include,

the order of events, preparation, and how to divide responsibilities.

- Make sure each of you has a clear picture of what the
other people want.
- If past holidays have had glitches, set your boundary for
what is acceptable to you and what isn't. For example, "I
need to start serving dinner on time. If you're not here
by seven, we'll start without you, and you can join us as
soon as you can."
- Look for ways to include the most important elements
for each person.
- Be clear about what you are committing to and what you
are not. Be sure you have a similar clear commitment
from the other person.

After the Holiday

- If your boundaries were disregarded, calmly and honestly discuss how and why this happened.
- If the other person made a genuine mistake, set your
boundary again clearly and directly. If *you* made a mistake, own up to it, apologize, and make appropriate
amends, if necessary.
- If the other person is unwilling or unable to adapt, or
seems to be playing games with you, decide how you
will do the next holiday with greater protection for your
boundaries. You may have to celebrate separately in
order to preserve the spirit of the holiday for yourself.
- Allow the relationship to have a learning curve. Cut
some slack if the holiday wasn't perfect, but the other
person made an effort. Express your appreciation for
their flexibility and willingness to adapt.

- Learn from any misunderstandings.
- Repeat the negotiation process several weeks before the next holiday.

WEDDINGS

The most important people at a wedding ceremony are the two people about to plight their troth. Regardless of family tradition, social standing, or social obligations to distant people, it's the couple's inauguration to their own marriage.

Of course, choices may be limited by financial restrictions—and it is important not to put yourself into financial difficulty for the sake of your own or someone else's wedding—but once financial limits are respected, remember that it's the substance, not the form, that matters most.

If your daughter wants to be married in a cowboy outfit, why not? You had your chance. It's her turn now. If the nuptial couple doesn't want to serve alcohol at the reception, don't bring alcohol to the event. If they don't want any gifts made from animal products, check labels before buying.

Control issues around weddings may be arising from the difficulty of taking in that this younger generation is embarking on adult life. Let go. Be graceful. Cry on your spouse's shoulder. The bride and groom are picking up their own reins. Let them.

BIRTHDAYS

The birthday person gets to set the boundaries for his own celebration. Pay attention to hints about gifts. Some families make a little hint basket for each member, in which they can drop pictures or ads or want lists throughout the year.

Respect preferences. Even though you'd be thrilled if every friend since kindergarten showed up for your fortieth birthday bash, your spouse might just grin and bear such a shindig. Surprises can be fun and a sign of your love, but keep them within the comfort limits of the person being surprised.

Know your person. Jim would love a roast. Tim would be embarrassed. Slim would feel exposed. Ken would be insulted. If in doubt, ask.

VALENTINE'S DAY

Although this holiday is for both lovers for the most part, women especially set a lot of store by Valentine's Day. This is not the time to get gruff and stand on your principles if your woman wants to be treated like a princess for one evening.

Think of it this way. You will get a lot of points for putting yourself out for this one holiday. For the twenty minutes it takes to make a reservation, order flowers, pick out a card, and tell her you have a surprise and she'll need to dress up a little, you will get credits for days. If you draw a blank about how to treat her like a princess, ask any woman.

A satisfactory Valentine's Day strengthens the integrity of an intimate relationship, while an unwillingness to consider a spouse's need to receive special treatment now and then can be a violation that stretches the fabric of the relationship.

BUT IT'S THANKSGIVING!

No occasion or holiday is reason enough for you to subject yourself to abuse. I can't count the times I've heard a client say, "Well, of course, I have to go spend the week with:

- my sexually inappropriate father
- critical mother
- drunken stepfather
- disregarding sister

After all, it's:

- Christmas
- Thanksgiving
- Mother's Day
- Leap Year
- The Anniversary of Manned Flight

Why should you spend your holiday being treated badly? For the sake of the someone else's holiday, is it okay for you to be disregarded, criticized, humiliated, sexually harassed, or exposed to the boring inanities of a drunk?

No! If you aren't able to set boundaries with these people yet, or if they aren't capable of respecting boundaries you set, you just plain don't have to go.

You get to have a wonderful holiday. You are not required to sacrifice it for someone who treats you badly just because you are related to them. Wrap up this book, stick a bow on it, send it to them as a present, and say, "When you understand Chapter _____, give me a call."

Other options are:

- "Dad, are you still drinking? You are? Okay, well, have a nice Christmas. I've got other plans this year."
- "Mom, you just criticized me three times in the first minute of our conversation. I don't want to spend a whole day with more of the same. I won't be there for Super Bowl Sunday."
- "Sis, I'll come to Thanksgiving dinner if you'll agree not to make any comments about my body, weight, or clothing. If you can do that, I'll come. But at the first comment, I'm out of there. What do you hear me saying?"

GIFTS

The fine art of gift giving can strengthen the boundaries of a relationship. A gift that fits its recipient enhances a relationship. A good gift communicates, "I care about you." A great gift communicates, "I know who you are." By taking a moment to think about your friend or loved one, you can pick a gift that says, "I know you. I know what you like and care about."

The closer you are to someone, the more important it is to give a gift that truly delights and pleases them, that they will use or enjoy. If you aren't able to imagine what that could be, ask them.

A message hits with more impact when it is wrapped in gift paper, because a gift sets up an expectation. We know to back up and put up some protection when someone is screaming at us, but when someone offers a pretty package, we lower our protection.

A gift opens us. We relax. In this opened state, the painful message behind a poorly chosen or inappropriate gift goes deeper.

Nevertheless, it's good to make allowances for people who love you dearly but just don't have much imagination. Since Dad's perpetual concern is for your protection, when you graduate from law school, he gives you a car jack. He truly means well and it comes from love, so you needn't be stung by it.

If someone close to you simply has not mastered the art of gift giving, give them a list of things you'd like to have, including sizes and preferred colors. In doing this you are saying, "Gifts outside this limit will strain a festive occasion and cast a shadow at a time when we could be strengthening our connection. Gifts within this limit will delight me and improve our relationship."

Cost is not as important as thoughtfulness. If your wife likes having her feet rubbed, ten cute handmade coupons for foot rubs might be appreciated more than expensive earrings.

Know what gifts would be a bomb. Most women would not like getting a vacuum cleaner for their birthday. I wonder if men get tired of getting socks and ties.

Giving a manipulative gift can harm a relationship. For example, Hortense always gave Lizbeth, her adult daughter, gifts that fit Hortense's expectations of Lizbeth. She wanted Lizbeth to join the Junior League and enter society, so she gave Lizbeth expensive clothes and jewelry that fit Hortense's lifestyle. But Lizbeth, who loved her job as a nurse at an inner-city clinic, wore jeans and T-shirts when she wasn't in uniform, and led a casual life. She had no use or room for her mother's presents, and the inherent pressure of such gifts drove a wedge between them.

Mitchell always gave his daughter clothes in the wrong size and style. He picked lovely things, but two sizes too small. Nancy took this as a message that he was critical of her weight. Plus, the clothes seemed more than a bit on the sexy side. It seemed just past the edge of appropriate, as if he wanted to see her dressed in a way that emphasized her sexuality.

DOESN'T THE THOUGHT COUNT?

It does. But if your gift is an attempt to control, persuade, manipulate, or disregard the other person, then *that* is the thought conveyed.

The importance of gift selection increases with the intimacy of a relationship. Among strangers, distant relatives, and neighbors, a gift that demonstrates, "I had a good thought about you and I was willing to expend some energy or money on your behalf" is a good gift. But the closer we are to someone, the more important a gift becomes, and the more personal it needs to be.

Aretha's husband, knowing she hates housework, would mess up if he gave her a mop or an iron. Since she loves basketmaking, a variety of basketry materials or a ticket to a basketry class would be a great gift.

A gift that misses big could even be a boundary violation. M. Scott Peck[1] writes of a family that gave their son the rifle his older brother had used to kill himself. This gift threatened more than the son's relationship with his parents. It was also a threat to the son himself. Even if they had some positive intent, they didn't make the effort to imagine the impact the gift would have on their surviving son.

---

[1] M. Scott Peck, *People of the Lie* (New York: Simon & Schuster, 1983), 47–69.

In making good relationships, we are challenged to imagine the impact of our behavior on others, to stretch our minds beyond the parameters of our inherent parochialness, our local perspective. Too much thought and responsibility for others becomes codependence and enmeshment. Too little becomes narcissism and excessive self-focus. We improve our own integrity, and that of our relationships, by finding a middle ground.

Gift giving is one way in which this middle ground is communicated. We protect our financial and time boundaries by not giving more money or time than we can afford, while making the effort to understand what matters to someone and picking a gift that contributes to their interests or joy.

Chapter 14

SEXUAL BOUNDARIES

Paul and Helen had been married eleven years. They had weathered difficult situations with persistence, had deep trust in their relationship, and knew each other well enough to answer questions barely started ["Did you get . . ." "Yes."].

Despite their intimacy, however, they still had a serious glitch in their relationship. Paul would be revved to enjoy a tumble with Helen, and she would be turned off by an overtly sexual approach. This is a relatively common problem between intimate partners.

One Saturday, Paul woke up sexually charged and said so to Helen. She said, "Not now, dear, I'm hungry. Maybe later." She thought, *I don't feel sexual toward you. We haven't seen each other for a week. The last time we were together, we had a big fight. I need to know you as a person again before I can open to you.*

Paul went through the day with the expectation that in the afternoon, Helen's best sexual time, they'd hit the hay. But Helen dreaded a sexual encounter and was thinking about how to gear herself up for it. Meanwhile she was also feeling lonesome, and a need to zone out.

After lunch, Paul threw himself into making a clever gadget for Helen to use in the kitchen. After lunch Helen said she needed time to herself and took a nap. When she woke up, the gadget was installed and it was wonderful.

Paul then turned to her eagerly. He said, "The entire time I was making this, I pictured diving into your luscious body. It really turned me on."

She said, "I need some time with you first."

His face fell. He felt angry and frustrated.

She tried to get Paul to talk about it. She knew that if they could have an intimate conversation, she could feel more sexual. She suggested several ways that would make it possible for her to feel closer to him.

But he was already too upset. He wasn't interested in talking or in responding to what she needed. He felt he'd been cheated.

The rest of their day was rough, full of little spats. When Helen tried to talk about it again later, they both had frayed tempers. Worse, Paul was in a mood to retaliate. She'd rejected him, he felt, so he rejected her attempts to heal the rift.

In nearly every intimate relationship, one partner is more sexually charged than the other. Making room for the needs of each person can be a challenge. Furthermore, nearly everyone alive has suffered some sort of violation to their sexuality.

Male sexuality is forced into strict channels at an early age. Many a teenage boy gets desperate for a sexual outlet, any sexual outlet. If his private way of taking care of his needs is ridiculed or restricted, he may seek relief from less healthy sources.

Females are often used sexually when they are young. Many a young woman finds herself pulled into a sexual encounter, thinking she herself is prized, only to discover that the ravenous male appetite would just as happily have dined on almost any female flesh.

We get set up early in life—even if we haven't been violated in more serious ways—to be incompatible. Harm done to us sexually affects us for a lifetime. We can heal much of the damage from the harm, but it may still influence our instinctive reactions to sexual situations.

In addition, male and female bodies have profound hormonal differences that create friction. The peak for male and female sexuality is separated by about twenty to twenty-five years. (Whose plan was that?) Males have a surge of testosterone in the morning, women a hormonal surge in the afternoon. After ejaculation, a male hormone is released that makes a man sleepy; at that same point, women often wake up. This is exactly the time at which a woman wants to be held and talked to. If the man goes to sleep, she feels abandoned.

A man is in a more vulnerable position before intercourse. He needs her and he wants to perform well. Many women feel more vulnerable after intercourse. She's surrendered something. She's allowed her body to be entered.

Women need to feel close in order to feel sexual. Men have sex to feel close. After a fight, a man turns to the woman to have sex. He's wanting sex to reestablish intimacy. She says, "Are you crazy? I don't feel sexual toward you. We just had a fight. All you ever think about is sex." [2]

---

[2] Ellen Friedman, *Light Her Fire* (Morton Grove, Ill.: Mega Systems, 1995).

PREPARATION FOR SEXUALITY

From an early age, boys are propelled by their own instincts to be physical. They test the limits of their physical endurance all the time, learning to use their bodies as they would an important tool. They gain catlike control over their movements.

Little girls are more likely to have experiences that teach them to separate from their bodies. Possibly 38 percent of adult women were sexually abused as children.[3] Such abuse causes girls, often unconsciously, to view their bodies as sources of danger. They learn to take a mind trip elsewhere whenever their bodies are being hurt.

Menstrual periods can be excruciatingly painful, provoking further detachment. Today we have sanitary products that don't hurt when we use them, but when I was a girl, our choices were limited, and the sanitary products could even be painful to wear. Imagine what it does to a woman's relationship with her body to know that once a month pain and discomfort will visit her for at least a couple of days, and perhaps as long as two weeks.

I occasionally ask female clients to mark a drawing of a human body to illustrate the parts of their bodies they can sense kinesthetically. An amazing number black out the entire area from the shoulders to the thighs. Some women draw a line at their necks, indicating that all their awareness is in their heads.

If a woman has been hurt early in her life through sexual activity, later even in a loving relationship with a skilled and

---

[3] Margaret Hyde and Elizabeth Forsyth, *The Sexual Abuse of Children and Adolescents* (Brookfield, Conn.: Millbrook Press, 1997).

thoughtful lover, she might detach instantly the moment she has pain. One second she's present, and the next, due to a little tweak or too much pressure, she's gone—and she may not know she's gone. The man is progressing and by the time she comes back to full awareness, he's much further along than she is. Unfortunately, women tend to endure this gap and make themselves hurry up, which perpetuates their own exploitation.

Women violate their own boundaries when they don't speak about their needs, or by enduring—out of love or expediency—sexual activity. Over time, a woman who does this is bound to lose interest in sex.

In the long run, it benefits both the man and the woman for her to be honest about what is happening to her as they share a sexual experience. It's tragic that so often couples get focused on performing rather than experiencing, losing the joy and wonderful connection that true lovemaking can bring.

The value of a committed relationship is that there is time for everyone's needs. A man will get more value in the long run if he is patient and thoughtful of his woman, if he ceases instantly any touch that causes pain, and if he gives some time for emotional connection before making physical moves.

A woman will find herself with a more involved man if she lets him have some times of pure sexual abandon (minus any pain, of course). Women can rev themselves up with thoughts and fantasies and sexual aids, so that they are both physically and emotionally ready for their men to play. Women can take responsibility for ensuring their own pleasure, not always leaving that job in the hands of the men.

Give and take, thoughtfulness, kindness, communication, and humor can all strengthen the intimacy of the relationship.

NEW SEXUAL BOUNDARIES FOR OUR CULTURE

If we could begin to raise children who are not sexually harmed, future couples would have less damage to overcome. This requires awareness and vigilance on the part of the adults in each family, to protect the children so that their boundaries aren't violated.

A third of abused children are victimized by older children or siblings.[4] Parents must be careful about leaving younger children in the care of older male children who are of an age to have sexual stirrings or curiosity. Only 5 percent of abusers are strangers and males are more likely to molest than females.[5] We warn children to be careful around strangers, but they need to be taught to say no to anyone, even a relative, who touches them or approaches them inappropriately. Parents and grandparents must take care not to leave children in the hands of anyone who does not seem safe.

A new approach would offer teenagers practical help. This would mean giving young men healthy ways to deal with their hormone-driven sexuality without preying on young women or children. This would also mean teaching young men to respect women, to accept no as an answer, and to care for others.

---

[4] Ibid.
[5] Dale Robert Reinert, *Sexual Abuse and Incest* (Springfield, N.J.: Enslow, 1997).

Young men *are* being taught how to give pleasure rather than just to take. And we are learning to teach young women to respect their bodies, to set limits, to avoid dangerous situations. We are teaching young women about young men's powerful sexual drives and how to protect themselves. We are going beyond clinical sexual education and talking about the strong feelings involved.

But we also need good men to take a stronger stand against rape, incest, and sexual exploitation. A shift in cultural attitude, one that sees exploitative behavior as wrong, can make a huge difference in increasing safety for women, and in helping everyone to have healthier sexual boundaries—and greater sexual intimacy.

CASUAL SEX

In the brief window between Victorian prudishness and the spread of AIDS, we had a sexual revolution. After a century of sexual denial, many of us tested boundaryless sexuality—nudity, multiple sexual partners, sexual exploration, and initial sexual encounters at younger ages.

Then, when serious disease and death became the consequences of mindless promiscuity, we rode the pendulum to a more balanced position. Today we are more open about sex, somewhat closer to the European acceptance of bodily appetites, and a great deal more knowledgeable about the sexual workings of the opposite gender. Couples who are dating are likely to bed earlier, and with less commitment to each other, than their counterparts of thirty years ago.

Still, our emotional processes may not be as casual as our physical actions imply. For many women, a sexual encounter creates a bond that feels torn if the man, afterward, disappears. What starts as insouciant entertainment for both people can become, after intercourse, a meaningful episode for the woman.

Sexual bonding that isn't accompanied by some foundation of familiarity with the other person can yield a chilly morning after. We are visited by the lonely realization that we have been intimate with a stranger whose values and ways are obscure to us.

I encourage my women readers to protect their boundary of emotional safety by giving a relationship some time to build before becoming sexually vulnerable. Let yourself be known, and let yourself know the other person, before jumping into the sack.

HEALTHY SEXUAL BOUNDARIES

We must keep good sexual boundaries to preserve our integrity. We must say no if a sexual experience is causing us pain or too much risk, either physically or emotionally. We must respect "no" the instant we hear it. It can be frustrating to stop, but to continue past a "no" destroys the other person's sexual safety with you.

We must take responsibility for our own pleasure, by saying what feels good, by asking for the touch we like, and by continuing to give guidance with words or gestures.

If your partner has been abused sexually, they may experience flashbacks or sorrow during sex. It can be so hard to stop when you are aroused, but an investment of kindness, patience, and care can ultimately bring you a wonderfully responsive sexual partner.

From Hollywood we've gotten the idea that passion progresses in a consistent line from the kiss to the postcoital cigarette. In real life, people pause in the middle to talk or rest, alternate being fast or slow, use words to guide their partner, play, laugh, cry, and express powerful love.

Chapter 15

GENDER BOUNDARIES

Luisa's story:

A few months before I was born, my father told my mother, "If the baby is a girl, I'm leaving you and you can take the baby with you; but if it is a boy, I'll never let him go."

They divorced before my first birthday. My mom took me, of course.

For the first part of my life, I had a wonderful, safe childhood. We lived with my grandparents, who did the lion's share of raising me. I had a grandfather, an uncle, a minister, and great-uncles who cared about me, loved me, and guided me. I could crawl on my uncle's lap, or be patted on the head by my grandfather, and know without words that I was protected. My grandfather taught me to fish and to handle tools and motors.

You'd think I'd never miss my father. After all, I'd never known him, except when I was too young to be conscious of him. I had three strong, loving men to father me. There was no experiental father gap in my life, yet I missed my father every single day.

I would dream about my father and long for him. I'd wonder what he looked like and why he never wanted to see me. I'd often pretend, as I walked home from school, that my father was waiting for me at home. As I approached our block, I'd look for him to see if he was walking to meet me.

When I was twenty-one I took the reins in my own hands. I went looking for him. I had saved hints for years from little comments my mother and grandmother let slip when they thought I wasn't paying attention, and I went searching for him. And I found him. Oh, what joy I felt, how filled out I felt when I first found him and had a face and eyes and limbs and form to fill out my imagination.

While she was still in the womb, Luisa was the target of a gender boundary violation. Her father would not value her because she was female. His subsequent behavior, once she was born, validated his first statement.

Luisa bore the consequences. As a child, the price she paid was constantly longing for him, experiencing the emptiness of not being connected with him.

Luisa's story continues:

I had believed that once I found my father, he would become a part of my life and that we'd be close from then on. As it turned out, I tried for another twenty years to interest him. I took up his hobbies, tried to achieve awards and recognition that would impress him, and tried to maintain routine contact with him.

I couldn't seem to overcome the chasm created by not growing up in his milieu. I didn't know the in jokes, the phrases, the habits of response that were typical to that side of the family. I sensed that words that were mild and loving to me were threatening and intrusive to him. I never ceased to be a foreigner.

Once Luisa met her father, their unfamiliarity with each other, their lack of common language, and a continued paucity of interest on his part created a gap that years of effort on her part could not cross.

Fathers aren't interchangeable with other men. Children's connection with their fathers grounds and centers them like nothing else.

Even in a good home with lots of loving people, a hole exists if the father isn't available. Note that as a child Luisa had never known her father, had never had contact with him. Her longing wasn't the kind that comes when someone you love leaves you.

The need for each parent is seemingly the material of our cells. Our atoms reach for connection with those who spawned us, and we want that connection as long as we live.

Brad's story:

I was always in trouble as a kid. It seemed that if I breathed, somebody'd yell at me. In fact that did happen. I was yelled at for breathing through my mouth and making too much noise. I was always too something—too loud, too messy, too dirty, too smelly.

I'd come in from playing and my mother would say, "Ugh, you smell." She didn't say it kindly, either. She always acted irritated with me.

I always had to do the worst chores. I'd have to muck out the barn. I'd have to walk through subzero temperatures with snow up to my knees to get some stray animal from across the field. My sisters would be inside, warm and laughing, doing their chores together. They had it so easy, in that warm house, while I was forced to be outside, alone and freezing.

Selma's story:

We had a big family—Catholic, you know—and I was the youngest. I had three sisters and two brothers. We lived in an area where there were lots of kids. When I didn't have to work in the store, I roamed all over the mountains, playing with my friends.

My brothers weren't getting very good grades, so my mother decided that my brothers needed to go to a more important school. We were doing okay, but we weren't rich. So, while Dad stayed in Silverton and ran his business, she dragged all us kids with her to Denver so that my brothers could go to an expensive school there for three years. She rented a place for us to stay. It put such a strain on us financially that Mom and Dad lost the house they were building.

Except for my brothers, the lives of all of us were smashed. I begged her to leave me with Dad. I could help him in his store and still have my circle of friends. I was doing well in our school, making good grades. I liked my teachers. I liked my life.

When she plunked me down in Denver, I couldn't seem to recover. I couldn't find a niche in the Catholic school where she put us girls. The neighborhood was stark and scary. We girls were afraid to play outside very far from home. It's as if a life of color turned suddenly to black and gray.

Eventually I got used to being passed over for the boys. I got used to the rest of the family being sacrificed to pour all the resources into them. I didn't even feel a flicker of dissonance when I wanted to learn accounting and was told girls had to be secretaries or teachers or nurses. I trained to be a secretary and was forty years old before I found out I had exceptional intelligence and could have made a lot of money.

In my family, the boys were more important than the girls. They were given all the opportunities, and as a result, today they all live in big houses and drive big cars and belong to the country club. They think they have a God-given right to tell me how to run my life, even now. They have the gall to criticize my house, when the reason I'm stuck in that little house is due to their guidance when I was a young adult.

It's taken me a long time to get over being bitter about it and to learn how to handle them when they still try to treat me like Cinderella, fit only to serve the men.

The fact is, the course of my life was set and limited for one reason only—I was born female.

Luisa's father had no interest in her because she was a girl. Brad's family treated him like a cinderfella. Selma's family nurtured the sons like hothouse flowers at great cost to themselves, and restricted the lives of the daughters so that the girls didn't even realize they had choices until late in life.

When a person is dismissed, rejected, denied opportunities, discriminated against, or undervalued because of their gender, it's a gender boundary violation.

FEMALE BOUNDARY VIOLATIONS

Sunny's story:

I come from generations of women who worshiped maleness. When my brother and I would visit my grandmother, she'd talk to him and give him treats. But she hardly noticed I was there.

"Buddy!" she'd say to my brother, "I just baked cookies. Come to the kitchen with me." And she didn't even say hello to me.

I'd trail after the two of them to the kitchen, 'cause I didn't know where else to go. She'd fix a plate of cookies and put it in front of him and pour him a glass of milk, and then catch sight of me, as if she was surprised I was there—even though I came through the door with him just ten minutes earlier.

"Oh, Sunny, you have a cookie, too." Then she'd get me milk and a cookie, but it was an afterthought, the skeleton of courtesy, not a sacrament of love, as it was for Buddy.

As we grew up, the same thing kept happening. Gathered at Christmas with the aunts and Gram, Buddy got a million questions about college and sports and, eventually, his job or his interests. All the boys in the family had their way paid to college. I worked hard to get scholarships and had jobs the whole time I was in college. None of the other girls in the family even tried.

No one cared that I was summa cum laude or that I got a grant to study vector populations in the desert. I was chosen out of thousands of applicants. I could have gotten nominated for a Nobel Prize and they'd have uttered an unenthusiastic, "That's nice, dear; now Buddy, what were you saying?"

I have heard countless stories of little girls set aside because they weren't male. The little boys in their families were valued, attended to, given opportunities, encouraged, and the little girls ignored or treated like cinderellas raised to serve the boys.

Today, in certain Middle Eastern and Asian countries, girl children are given away, sold, or abandoned, in order to save the family's or nation's resources for the boy children. When American parents, desperate for a child, can't find a baby to adopt in the United States, they can, at great expense, go through a broker in Asia who will obtain for them a female child. It is the females who are expendable.

What happens to little boys raised in such a culture or household? They grow up having been fortified with advantages, yes, but is there any other consequence? When a family favors the male children, they grow into men who have a sense of entitlement, and an unconscious belief in their superiority to women.

And what about the little girls? Believe me, they notice if they are excluded from attention, conversation, opportunities, affection, and activities in favor of the boys. Without words or articulation, such discrimination registers at a subliminal level, and many little girls then automatically close the door to a wide range of options and possibilities. Without conscious awareness, they accept profound limitations.

Preferential treatment of either male or female children produces adults who will have some difficulty in their relationships with the opposite sex. Men and women can't possibly enter into marriage as equals if their programming has instilled attitudes of superiority or inferiority.

Marrie and Rashid were good people. Rashid was clever, ethical, and funny. Marrie was warm, loving, and generous. In every way they exemplified a modern, well-adjusted couple. Rashid was a feminist. Marrie loved men. There was no trace of gender prejudice in the speech or actions of either person. They came to me because of Marrie's problem. She was depressed.

I quickly saw that Marrie's self-esteem was in the basement. I asked her to do a task, a small one, and she apologized before she even started, telling me not to expect much from her. The challenge caused her so much anxiety that she started to shove it away, afraid to even try. Yet she did it perfectly, and when I pointed that out, she said it was a fluke that she did it well. I began to point out other areas in her life where she had demonstrated competence. In every case, she minimized it.

In sessions, she would often build Rashid up, complimenting him, describing an achievement of his. He would soak it up like a sponge. His spirit would grow larger. He loved and needed her appreciation. But I never saw him compliment her or build her up. I did see him watch coldly, and with an air of impatience, as she fumbled in her purse to find the keys or checkbook.

As I autopsied the course of their marriage, I uncovered a pattern of long, slow erosion in Marrie's self-regard. She had entered the marriage competent, strong, and with big dreams of her own. She put those dreams aside as children came, and by the time they had the resources for her to get the education to fulfill her dream, she had lost her ability to risk.

As a child, Rashid had been subtly treated like a crown

prince. In adulthood, he was not aware that he held deep beliefs that his perspective, decisions, and thoughts were superior to Marrie's.

Rashid soon lost interest in therapy, continuing to see Marrie as the one having the problem. Marrie, too, left therapy after only a few months, saying that she was needed at home and didn't like to use so much of the family's financial resources just for her little problem.

An attitude, like water, leaks out to dampen one's actions and responses. It comes through. It has an effect, in countless invisible ways.

MALE GENDER VIOLATIONS

Anthes's story:

> I was shut out as a boy. My mother and sisters belonged to some female club that excluded me from its warmth and color.
>
> They weren't obvious about it—they loved me and looked out for me at school and all—but they would get into a flurry of conversation about clothes or boyfriends or how they were going to compete at the county fair, and I'd be on the sidelines, waiting to be interesting to them.
>
> I began to create my own life out of books and studying. Gradually I created my own separate niche that fascinated me. They teased me, and it was a kind of loving attention, though it spotlighted me as eccentric. I began to get some identity from being eccentric, and I seemed to continue to be different from others everywhere I was.

In high school, I was odd because I studied and cared about doing well. In college I was odd because I had liberal views and wouldn't cheat. I've been the odd man out in business, too, because I keep accurate expense logs. I don't pad my budget, I won't cheat a client or the company, and I work the full amount of hours expected of me.

I don't comment on any of this to my fellow workers or do anything to stand out, but I'm not included as a member of the Ol' Boys' Club. I'm not invited for drinks after work. I'm not told dirty jokes, which is okay because I find them distasteful anyway. I'm not invited to the ball games or impromptu parties.

I've found an internal satisfaction from living cleanly, but it seems like, as far back as I can remember, I've been lonesome.

Anthes was a victim of a subtle gender violation. He was excluded, not because he was male, but because he wasn't female. In a predominantly female household, he wasn't discriminated against, but he was left out. The women and girls banded together around their female interests, while he dangled as a family appendage—loved, but not drawn into the action.

Children need to belong, to be made a part of their family's interests and activities. Leaving out children because of gender influences them in important and lasting ways—for the course of their entire lives.

Crosby's story:

When I was a kid, I couldn't do anything right. I ate too fast. I ran around too much. I fidgeted. I was too messy. I tracked up the floor. I got my clothes too dirty. I got into too many scrapes.

My sister was perfect. She was neat. She kept her room tidy. She never spilled anything. She got good grades.

She could come into the living room in her pajamas while Mom and Dad were watching television and cuddle into my mom's lap, and my mom would stroke her hair or rub her back. I tried to cuddle with Mom once and she pushed me away. I didn't try that again.

I have an exceptional male relative who, when he was a boy, said, "How come my sister gets held and I don't?" He woke us all up, and we realized we'd made the unconscious error of thinking that we should keep more of a physical distance with him because he was a boy. From then on, we gave in to our own natural instinct to hold and cuddle him. He lapped it up all the way through high school. When I saw this dear child, at 250 pounds and with linebacker shoulders, curled up on the couch with his head in his grandmother's lap, having his head stroked, I realized how much he jarred us loose from unconscious, counterproductive cultural attitudes.

ADULT GENDER VIOLATIONS

Biological Boundaries

Let's take a simple example of a biological gender difference. Estrogen makes one feel colder. A woman's basal body temperature drops in the estrus phase of her menstrual cycle and she will chill more easily. Men have a higher metabolism. They burn fat more readily and they are generally warmer.

Throughout my lifetime I've heard women disparaged by men for being cold. But a man who mocks his wife for feeling chilly is mocking the very process that makes her womanly, that allows her to conceive, that gives her a womanly shape. In short, he is ridiculing her for a biological process over which she has no control, and because of which he receives gifts he could never get from a man.

Hot flashes are also culturally mocked, even by women. A hot and sweaty man is usually considered sexy, but a hot, sweaty woman, no. A hot woman, a cold woman—both made sport of? Not okay.

"Hey, baldy, the glare from your dome is blinding me." Men have no control over hair loss. This is a genetically mediated process.

"She's too tall." "He's too short." How *could* a woman be too tall or a man too short? A person has no control over how long their bones will grow. Neither men nor women can choose their body type, their height, or their metabolism.

"Sex is all he cares about." "We were fighting and he started touching me! What a jerk." "Every time we hug, he starts feeling me up. He's completely insensitive." When women are with other women, it's not uncommon for them to belittle the sexuality of their husbands. Both parties lose when women relate to a man's sexuality in a largely negative way. Many lack understanding that a man's physicality is hormonally induced, a normal part of the male system.

All such disparaging remarks and putdowns are boundary violations. Indeed, whenever a person is mocked or ridiculed for their biology or gender, it's a boundary violation.

CULTURAL VIOLATIONS

For the rest of this chapter I'm going to depart from the general tone of this book to talk about a problem that, because of its near invisibility, could continue to sneak up on us and limit our own choices and those of coming generations.

In nearly every corner of the world, there exists a gap between two groups. As group A gathers benefits and gains access to its rights, it does so at the expense of group B.[6] Men gain advantages at the expense of women. Throughout history and in many parts of the globe, this gap causes uncounted boundary violations toward females based solely on gender. Women and men have been fighting to close this gap for at least three hundred years in various countries. Being educated about this problem is one way to help close the rift.

When an entire culture collaborates in its view of a gender, the children will absorb this perspective and carry the consequential limitations, privileges, and attitudes into adulthood.

If Mary, as a baby, is pulled from her mother's breast because her older brother wants a sip, both children will learn their place in the scheme of things and not question it. A toy taken from the girl child and presented to the boy child, girls taught to serve their brothers dinner before they can sit and eat as well, children watching the mother work nonstop while the father rests and is served, grow up not setting their own boundaries but buying the culture's pattern.

For millennia females in nearly every country in the world have been born into a second-class existence, into a template that has sanctioned female gender violation, violation that

---

[6] Kathleen Barry in *Encyclopedia Americana,* International ed., vol. 29, s. v., "Women's Rights."

has extended even as far as culturally approved sexual abuse and exploitation.

"12% of the females born worldwide are missing, uncounted, uncountable, many of them victims of female infanticide. . . . Women presently work twice as many hours as men for one-tenth the income."[7]

In Britain, until 1882, when a woman married, all that had been hers became the property of her husband. If she owned jewels, land, or a mansion, at marriage, he was now the owner. He owned their children. Married women in America still did not have property rights as of 1890.[8]

In a few parts of the world, some females became conscious enough not only to question the traditional order, but to defy it. When this movement began—almost two centuries ago—these few couragous women were vilified even by other women. The idea of suffrage for women gained slow momentum.

Guess how many years it took, from the first introduction of the topic, for the first country to grant women the right to vote?

1. 20
2. 50
3. 70
4. 100

The first nation to grant women the vote did so in 1893. The first book on the subject was published in 1792.

Can you guess in which order the following countries or

---

[7] Ibid.
[8] Anne Perry, *Bethlehem Road* (New York: Fawcett Books, 1991)

provinces allowed women to vote? Britain, Switzerland, United States, Kuwait, New Zealand, France, USSR, Quebec, Saskatchewan, India, Nigeria, Brazil, Japan, Wyoming.

Here is the order in which the vote was granted:

1. Wyoming (1869)
2. New Zealand (1893)
3. Saskatchewan (1916)
4. USSR (1917)
5. Great Britain (1918—women had to be over the age of 30)
6. United States (1920)
7. Brazil (1932)
8. India (1935)
9. Quebec (1940)
10. France (1944)
11. Japan (1945)
12. Nigeria (1960)
13. Switzerland (1971)
14. Kuwait (Not yet)

If you are surprised that French women waited seventy years after the women in Wyoming to have a political voice, or that Indian and Brazilian women had a ballot nearly forty years before Swiss women, it only shows how little you were taught about women's history.

At least once a week I go to my encyclopedias for a fact that relates more to women than men, and I'm astounded at how often the reference I seek isn't in print in books or in widely used computer reference programs. Ignorance of women's history and difficult access to information about women are other ways women are violated culturally, another subtle way the culture truncates female experience.

It isn't that men are limiting the references chosen for computer encyclopedias or that male professors who write the texts for print encyclopedias are deliberately withholding information about women. It's that they themselves haven't been educated about women. Women's achievements are a blank in their own minds. Not having been exposed to information about female ingenuity, courage, or heroism, they don't know these exist.

Cultural violations are hard to see. The culture we live in is like the sea to a fish. Although it surrounds us, it is so much the fabric of our lives that it is invisible to us. The more aware we can be and the further we can expand our perspective, the better our chances for noticing when we are being treated by a man or woman with an attitude—that females are less than males.

Paying attention to what happens to women all over the world—educating ourselves about the history of women—opens our eyes and minds to the subtle attitudes that are still influencing the treatment of women.

We are but one generation removed from the movement in which women liberated themselves from traditional roles, and women still bump their heads on the glass ceiling, still don't receive equal pay and promotion, still aren't proportionally represented in Congress, local government, or management, and still are patronized by employers, doctors, and other professionals.

Studies show that women entering the emergency room with heart attacks are more likely to be viewed as exaggerating their symptoms, with consequential delays in receiving appropriate treatment. "Women [are] less likely to receive a kidney transplant, less likely to have their lung cancer diagnosed, and less likely to have cardiac catheterization ordered when symptoms indicate it. Medical research has historically been structured around males, and resulting diagnostic and treatment models are often inappropriate for women."[9] As of 1990, only 13.5 percent of the $6 billion budget of the National Institutes of Health was spent on studies devoted to women's health issues exclusively.[10]

Girls only eight or ten years old have already absorbed the culture's message that they should be thin and believe they should be on a diet, even if their size is objectively healthy and average. Anorexia and bulimia among teenage girls are rampant. These female children are acting out the culture's emphasis on female beauty as the primary source of feminine power—a message reinforced subliminally in nearly every movie. Even in cartoons, the female worth rescuing is attractive and feminine while the witch has features that are somehow distorted and aggressive.

FIGHTING CULTURAL VIOLATIONS

What can men and women do with their anger at these and other cultural boundary violations? We can set new boundaries. We can take care that male and female children are shown a wider view of women.

Some of the following suggestions do depart from most of

---

[9] John M. Smith, MD, *Women and Doctors* (New York: Atlantic Monthly Press, 1992).
[10] Susan R. Johnson and Gloria A. Bachmann, in *Encyclopedia Americana*, International ed., vol. 29., s. v., "Women's Health."

the boundary setting examples in the rest of the book. These go beyond saying, "No," or "Pay attention to this thing that is important to me."

When it comes to cultural gender violations, we must set boundaries in a wider way, by influencing the culture. Increasing your own consciousness, promoting increased consciousness for others—particularly children—and supporting organizations that promote changes in cultural attitudes or that create conditions in which girls are assisted in going beyond traditional female limits are the actions required if we are to influence the setting of a cultural boundary.

If we leave it to individuals, alone, without the support and commerce of other women and men, to influence cultural change just through the setting of individual boundaries in daily circumstances, we will wait a long time for the culture to be influenced. Certainly, girls and young women will not benefit quickly.

As more women are empowered, as girls are empowered early enough to have wider choices, a wave of boundaries spreads throughout the culture, and we come naturally to be intolerant of discrimination. We only have to look at the improvements for women since the 1970s to see the truth of this. North American women entering the new century are much more likely to perceive and object to gender violations such as patronizing treatment or cracks about female logic than women of the 1950s who would have joined in and laughed off such insults.

We can't, however, afford to rest on our laurels. Women are a long way from parity with men when it comes to the wealth and power structure in our country. Women's thoughts and contributions are still dismissed, just much more subtly.

I was in a store in Chicago recently, a store that specializes in maps and items for travelers. As I looked at a case of miniature doodads, an imposing man from a Middle Eastern country entered my space. He stepped much too close to me with his eyes on the case and I understood his intent was to bully me out of his way.

Had this happened twenty-five years ago I would have moved without thinking about it and without being conscious that I was joining in his assumption that he had more of a right to stand where he wanted than did I. Had it happened thirty years ago, I might have giggled apologetically and said, "Excuse me," as I moved out of his way.

But it happened now, so I understood the dynamics of the situation immediately. These are the very subtle types of interchanges that still happen among the unwary and that can be caught only if we stay alert.

Thus the following suggestions are more global than those in the rest of this book. We must know how to influence the culture positively and we must stay awake.

PARTICIPATING IN SETTING CULTURAL BOUNDARIES

1. Remember that the advances in female parity are recent. The women's liberation movement occurred in the seventies. (And there are still women who would be embarrassed to be called feminists.) We cannot afford to be complacent about two decades of improvement when we contrast that to at least 5,000 years of female oppression. We must continue to expand our consciousness so that we can catch subtle instances of gender violations and stop them.

2. Remember that really striking advancements are con-

fined to small parts of the world. Vast populations of women still live and die with truncated choices. Women in certain Eastern European countries have been deliberately and horribly raped as military policy and as an attempt at genocide. We can contribute to movements that provide shelter, counseling, and legal relief for these women.[11]

Empowering and providing assistance to women who have been harmed by men sets a limit by demonstrating our unwillingness to let women stay in the trauma caused by those conditions. It puts our outrage into a form that does some good. It says to the trammeled sister, "Here's a hand up. I pay attention that this was done to you."

3. Promote self-esteem for girls. Teaching women's place in history makes girls proud and improves how boys view women. Encourage your local schools to add curriculum and fund resources that help kids think about women's lives. The National Women's History Project[12] has wonderful inexpensive resources and kits for teachers to use at all school levels as well as books and posters that families can use at home.

Boys and girls that view women differently grow up into men and women who won't tolerate gender oppression.

4. Support organizations that provide empowering experiences for girls such as the Girl Scouts and the YWCA. Some youth organizations that were once exclusively for boys have opened their rolls to girl membership. These clubs can also be valuable, but boys and some leaders in those organizations may still carry subtle cultural attitudes that limit what girls will try to do.

---

[11] An example is Women for Women in Bosnia, PO Box 9733, Alexandria, VA 22304.
[12] 7738 Bell Road, Windsor, CA 95492-8518, (707)838-6000.

Even today, there are places where the organizations for boys receive more funding for their programs than organizations for girls. Call your community fund drive and check the allocations to boy and girl youth organizations. If they are unequal, protest. Give your money directly to the organization rather than to the fund drive. (Sometimes the girls will be portrayed in fund advertising even though their allocation has been eliminated. If they say they have a per capita allocation, in other words that they give more to organizations that have more kids signed up, point out that additional funding allows for expanded services that then attract greater membership.)

Girls in strictly female clubs are more likely to hold responsible positions, are more likely to share their ideas, and have higher self-esteem. They are more inclined to believe that they have options and that they can take risks. Girls who are in Girl Scouts, for example, are more likely to take leadership positions in other situations, such as at school or at church, and to enter leadership roles as women.

5. Don't let yourself be violated. If your doctor doesn't take you seriously, switch doctors. If an exam hurts, say so. Ask for a gentler approach. If you are in extreme straits, insist on appropriate and vigorous help. If a professional treats you like the little woman, fire him.

6. Look at your life. If you are a woman, what have you avoided doing because you thought you couldn't because you were female? How have you limited your own experiences because of attitudes instilled in you? Talk with other women. Get support for extending yourself. Do the things you want to do.

If you are a man, can you identify situations in which you advanced at the expense of a woman?

THE BIG PICTURE

Men have paid a bigger price than they know for their privileges and power. Men have been sought, not for themselves, but for what they can acquire or achieve. Men have been fooled and ensnared by subtle calculation, locked in relationships based on power plays and manipulation rather than true, honest, respectful connection.

The great war between the sexes is repeated in our internal war against our own mix of femaleness or maleness. As we shift in our treatment and perspective on the opposite sex, we shift in our acceptance of ourselves as well. As we gain acceptance for our own opposite sex characteristics, we respond more positively to the other gender.

Man and woman must achieve full partnership if the planet is to survive.[13] When the great thinkers of our time make this statement, they are speaking literally, not metaphorically. The planet Earth is in trouble, and the problems of the people on Earth are also serious, and it will take all of us working together to pull ourselves through the crisis that is at hand.

We have violated the boundaries of the natural world and it will take cooperation to fix the harm we've done. We can no longer afford to lose the contributions of any group of people be they different in race, gender, sexuality, religion, culture, or heritage.

---

[13] Jean Houston, "Laughter of the Gods," lecture presented at Mystery School for Hollyhock Centre, Cortes Island, BC, 1995.

Chapter 16

DIVORCE BOUNDARIES

Even three years after her divorce, Magda Coupe could not feel safe. Despite a protection order, her ex-husband still patrolled her block. When she started dating, a glance behind her date's car would show Mel's beat-up black truck a few cars back. She'd occasionally wake in the night to his hammering on the front door.

When Mel had his day with their son, Tommy would return smeared with candy, arms full of expensive gifts, chattering about all the questions Daddy asked about Mommy. Magda did everything she could to preserve Tommy's respect for his father. Mel did everything he could to turn Tommy against his mom.

She couldn't be sure how far Mel's rage would go. He had nearly killed her when they were married, yet she couldn't afford to uproot Tommy and run. All her assets were in the house and she had enough from her job to live one week at a time. She felt trapped in a nightmare.

There are too many stories of a parent (most of the time a woman) in this situation. They have had to divorce to save their life and possibly their children's. Meanwhile, they may continue to be the target of their ex-partner's rage.

Unfortunately, there are still judges who take lightly a woman's need to have legal protection from a violent ex-partner. In some areas, the typical police response to a woman's cry for help from a stalking ex is so tardy that women stop calling.

Too often children are used to control an ex-spouse. Departing fathers use their superior economic positions to entice their children to greener pastures. Ex-husbands leave ex-wives so destitute, the women are forced to scratch out a meager existence while completing an education and still providing loving care for their children.

Mothers have clutched their children possessively, allowing only cursory attention from perfectly good fathers. Children have pined for calls or visits from a departing parent, who seemingly shook off the past from themselves like dust from their shoes.

Love your child more than you hate your departing spouse. Remember that your child needs the love of both parents, so long as they can provide responsible care.

With the divorce rate approaching 67 percent, we need a divorce ethic. You can have an honorable divorce, one in which good boundaries protect the emotional, physical, and financial integrity of all who are affected by it.

AN HONORABLE DIVORCE

1. Put the children first. Marital conflict affects even babies, who have difficulty returning to physiological calm after being upset.[14]

---

[14] John Gottman, PhD, *Clinical Manual for Marital Therapy* (Seattle, Wash.: 1999).

2. Don't use the children to get at your ex-spouse. Children of a contentious divorce lose four years from their life span. If they themselves eventually divorce, they lose eight years.[15]

3. Don't discredit or undermine the other parent.

4. Divide assets fairly.[16] Leave neither parent so destitute that they must sacrifice themselves for their children's care.

5. Do nothing to threaten, harm, or endanger the children—or the other parent.

6. Seek help to handle your anger or rage.

7. Do not stalk the other parent.

8. Get help in accepting that your lives are now separate.

9. Protect the children from a truly dangerous parent.

10. Let the children stay in contact with a good parent.

11. Be a good parent yourself and stay in contact with your children.

12. Grieve.

13. Let go.

14. If you've been through three or more unsuccessful significant relationships, get help. Find out how you are keeping yourself trapped in a revolving door.

What an Honorable Divorce Looks Like

Cliff and Tara Graymeyer divorced after seven years of marriage. They had a five-year-old boy, Billie. They sold their

---

[15] John Gottman, PhD, "A Scientifically Based Marital Therapy," lecture delivered in Seattle, Wash., 1999.
[16] Kathleen Miller, *Fair Share Divorce* (Bellevue, Wash.: Miller Advisors, 1995).

house and bought a duplex. Cliff lived on one side, Tara on the other. Billie could run from one side to the other to be with either parent.

It was hard on each of the adults when the other one started dating, but they bore it as a willing price so that Billie could have the fullest possible childhood. These wonderful parents carried the entire consequences of their decisions so that their son's security and health would be protected.

Chapter 17

POSSESSION BOUNDARIES

When Clarene married Ernesto, she drove a humble little compact car—a bit worn, but quick and perky. It suited her exactly. It never broke down, it fit into nearly any parking space, and was as agile as a gazelle.

Ernesto had a thing against the car. He began a campaign to replace it. It had no class whatsoever. The dent over the right headlight made it look loopy. The side was pushed in a bit and the bumper hung crooked.

Clarene loved her car. It was hers. It was the first car she'd bought out of money she'd made at her first jobs. It represented independence to her. She felt good driving it. She felt good about herself driving it.

Ernesto talked about his professional image and how unsuitable it was for her to drive such a battered vehicle. It reflected badly on him, he said. He wanted to buy her a nice car. He wanted her to live like a princess.

Eventually Clarene felt that she was being unnecessarily stubborn. It seemed so important to Ernesto, and a car was just a thing, after all. She gave in.

He got her a polished, sedate sedan. He insisted on elegant black. It drove, in her opinion, like a huge coffin. Its boundaries were too far from her own edges. She felt isolated from the world while she was driving.

She never felt comfortable in that car. She missed her old car, but it was gone forever. She had let him take it from her, and she regretted it for years.

Marie treasured the rocking chair that her mother had been rocked in as an infant. When her husband, Stan, would hit her, threaten her, or demean her, she'd restore herself by nestling in the rocker with an afghan, a book, and a cup of tea. In their small house it was her private preserve. She'd feel her grandmother embracing her from the grain of the wood and she'd remember that she had been loved by the women of her family.

One year Marie went to visit her daughter, Naomi, five hundred miles away in Vancouver. Stan didn't like Naomi. She wasn't his daughter and was openly disdainful of his drinking and his treatment of her mother.

When Marie came back home, it took her a while to figure out what was missing. It was when she was seeking comfort after one of Stan's episodes that she realized her rocking chair was gone.

For once she confronted him, despite the danger of it. "Where is my chair?"

"I donated it to Goodwill. You're always moping about the poor. I did it for you."

She went immediately to Goodwill, but it was gone. They couldn't trace it.

Sadly, I've heard many stories like this. A man or woman enters matrimony with some treasured possession from the past—a car, an heirloom, a set of dishes, a pet, a doll, an old ratty desk. But their new mates seem to have a need to break their attachment to the object. Out of a desire to be a good spouse, and because of the pressure exerted on them, they relinquish the possession—to their great and long-lasting regret. Occasionally, as in Marie's case, their partners dispose of the object without their consent.

When someone gets rid of anything they know you treasure without your consent, they are committing a boundary violation. They are also demonstrating that they will scapegoat you in service to their own rage, hostility, or insecurity. An assault to your treasure is an assault directed at you. It's a deliberate infliction of emotional pain, used in order to control or punish you.

The things we treasure contribute to our sense of self. They may represent our heritage, history, genealogy, friendships, times of joy or innocence, memories, achievements, or self-discovery. When we let someone take such an item from us, we lose more than the object; we also give ourselves and the other the message that we cannot protect what is our own. We are diminished and we lose personal power.

If your partner pressures you to relinquish a treasure, look to the larger issue. Refuse to argue about the item. Take a clear stand that you want to keep it, you will keep it, and it is nonnegotiable.

Then, ask your mate to talk about what it represents to them. If they have difficulty answering—or if their answer is less than reasonable—it's probably a good idea to insist on marriage counseling, for your partner will likely do other things to try to control you.

This is an issue that looks like a relationship problem, but it is really a form of attack, a way for someone to feel safe or powerful. Their anxiety or fear is projected outward, into some object outside themselves, in order to deal with some internal discomfort.

Giving up the thing you treasure will not really fix things for your partner, because no matter how much power they get over other people, their inner discomfort will still return. We can't fix our inner issues by making someone else change.

EXAMPLE—SETTING BOUNDARIES WITH SOMEONE WHO PRESUMES TOO MUCH

Maisie and Gina were roommates in college. Maisie wanted to wear a pair of lacy panties to the Homecoming dance under her gown. When she couldn't find them in her lingerie drawer, she began tearing through other drawers and cabinets. She couldn't find them.

The next day, when she did her laundry, she found them. This was a mystery because she only wore them on special occasions, and the last such event had occurred months before. Later she mentioned the whole situation to Gina.

"I wore them," Gina said.

"You what?" Maisie responded, disbelieving.

"I wore them. I've been too busy to do laundry. I was out, so I looked in your drawer. They were pretty, so I borrowed them."

"That's not okay," said Maisie. "First of all, I want you to ask before you wear any of my things. Second, I don't lend my underwear. It's too personal. Not only that, those undies are special to me. I only wear them for special occasions. Now you've changed their specialness. You've changed how I feel about them."

"Good grief." Gina flopped on her bed and stuck out her lip. "It's only a pair of panties. I'll get you another pair at Kmart if it means so much to you."

"That's not the point. If you can't understand what I'm saying here, that in itself is important."

"I can't wait to tell Dawn about this."

"If you're going to spread this around the dorm, I'll ask for a new roommate. I'm not going to be threatened by gossip when all I'm doing is sticking up for myself. It isn't selfish to protect things that matter. I get to choose what is important to me. If you can't respect that, I can't be your roommate."

Borrow clothing only if you have permission, and even if you have general permission, make an additional specific request if the item you'd like to use is intimate, special, expensive, or very personal.

PRIVACY BOUNDARIES

Zoe's mom came to visit. Zoe still had to work, so her mother stayed home during the day, and then they'd have a nice meal and the evening together.

As Zoe carried out the trash cans one evening, the lid came off. She was astounded to see a teddy bear and shoe boxes in the can. The shoe boxes held mementos that had been stored in her closet.

She pulled those items out and then searched through all the garbage, finding some childhood story books and a diary she'd kept in college. It had been intact but now it had a broken lock. She was so furious that she had to sit and compose herself before gathering her treasures and marching back to the house.

"Mother," she said firmly, her voice revealing her appropriate anger, "what have you been doing while I've been at work?"

Her mother looked up from the TV. "I just sorted out your closets and drawers, dear. You have too much stuff."

"Am I twelve, Mother?"

She laughed. "Hardly."

"Actually, it would even be wrong to do this to a twelve-year-old. Mother, you had no right to go through my closets or drawers. You have no right to throw out my things. You are not allowed to read my diaries or journals."

"I don't know what you're so upset about. Those are just childhood things."

"They're memories, Mother. It's a part of my history and I get to choose what to keep from those times."

"There's a *Lucy* rerun you'd love to see."

"Mother, pay attention. Do not *ever* go through any of my things again. If you can't stay out of my stuff, tell me right now."

"I'm just interested in you, dear. I like to see what you have."

"Do you have any concept of what is private and what isn't?"

"Well, of course, I'm not a fool."

"Do you know that you violated my privacy?"

"You're my daughter. We don't have secrets."

"Let me make this really clear. I am not willing to put padlocks on my closets and drawers, and I can't be worried while I'm at work about what you're doing here, so tomorrow, I'll take you to either the senior center or the library, your choice. I'll pick you up when I'm through working."

"That's not comfortable for me, dear."

"That's too bad. I can't trust you because you don't even know what you did."

"I don't know why you're making such a big thing out of this."

"I am so angry, it's taking everything I've got to stay respectful and clean," said Zoe. "Tomorrow you are not staying here, and I don't know when I'll be able to risk leaving you here alone, so perhaps you can think about places you'd like to stay while I'm working."

"I think I'd rather just leave early and go back home."

"If you'd cut short the visit rather than be willing to understand what you've done, that's your choice. It's a great disappointment to me that you'd prefer to go instead of admitting that you've violated my privacy, but, as I said, that's your choice. I've got to make a call. Think about what your definite decision is going to be and let me know later."

Reading an adult's journal, going through someone's private things, reading another person's letters—these are all boundary violations. We all need to be able to count on the integrity of our privacy, for this is one of the ways we restore ourselves.

Mementos, treasures, closets, and drawers are personal. They are not to be invaded by others, not to be sorted through or discarded without permission.

The only normal exception is if a departing spouse, partner, roommate, or adult child has ignored deadlines for getting their things out of a no-longer-shared space. We are not required to be the permanent custodian of the archives of a grown child or an ex-partner.

Another exception is when the space or objects belong to someone who has died or who has lost their mental faculties, and you are responsible for sorting out their affairs.

SETTING BOUNDARIES ON EXPLOITATION

Langley borrowed Sven's lawnmower and returned it covered with grass and low in gasoline. Sven gritted his teeth, serviced the mower, and said nothing when Langley borrowed it again. Of course it came back as dirty as before. Finally Sven said, "Langley, after you use my mower, please replace the gas and clean the blades and engine."

"Sure thing," said Langley with a friendly wave as he headed back to his place.

The next time Langley returned the mower, it had been swiped once with a cloth. Big clumps of grass had been brushed off, but the blades still had green paste where grass had mushed up next to the housing. The gas indicator showed half as much gas as it had had when Sven let him take it.

When Langley came to borrow it again, Sven asked, "Langley, do you know how to maintain a mower?"

Langley said, "Sure. I took care of mine just fine till it stopped running for some reason."

Sven felt stuck. If he tried to teach Langley now, it would seem as if he didn't believe him. Still, he pushed himself to say more. "Well, however you treated your own mower, here's what I do with mine." Sven explained step by step how maintenance should be done.

Langley agreed cheerfully and went off with the mower. It came back a little better this time, but plenty of green gunk was stuck to the housing and the gas was almost gone.

Sven told Langley he wouldn't be able to lend him his mower again.

Langley asked if he could borrow Sven's weedeater.

What do you think?

1. Sven should have tried one more time to explain this whole thing to Langley.
2. Sven should lend the weedeater.
3. Sven should offer to cut Langley's grass. He's too anal about keeping his mower clean.
4. Sven has already done too much explaining before taking a stand.

I'd go with option 4. Sven has already put far more effort into this situation than is appropriate given Langley's disregard. Sven's first clue was the first time Langley returned the mower without cleaning it or replacing the gas. Perhaps Langley was ignorant about the advantages of cleaning a mower, but an adult should already know to replace any consumables he's used, whether it's the gas in a machine or the half cord of firewood he used for a backyard bonfire. We don't exploit a friend's generosity by letting them be out of pocket for something that benefits us.

How could Sven have set a limit the first time Langley returned the mower?

"Langley, you forgot to refill the gas tank of the mower. Bring me a half can of gas the next time you want to borrow it. And I need it to come back clean next time. If it doesn't that will be the last time I'll lend it to you."

Should Sven explain mower maintenance in detail at this point? No. Langley has already revealed himself as someone who uses people. A person who had simply forgotten about the gas would respond with something like, "Holy smoke, I told myself to refill the gas tank and just forgot. I'll bring it right over. But honestly, Sven, it looks clean to me. What else needs to be done?"

This response shows an interest in keeping things equitable. It also demonstrates that Langley will take responsibility for finding out what he doesn't know.

We sometimes fall into the trap of thinking we should have explained all our expectations in advance—and, since we didn't, we don't now have the right to ask for something different. It's as if we see ourselves at fault for not anticipating anything that could have happened, rather than hold the other person accountable for understanding certain basics about not exploiting us. In short, we may be so fair to the other person that we end up being unfair to ourselves.

A clue that you're doing too much in a relationship is if you find yourself teaching the other person the same thing over and over. Sven kept teaching Langley about mower maintenance. Sven was missing the big picture—that Langley *didn't care* about Sven's preferences regarding his mower. Langley was interested in getting away with as much as possible.

You *always* have the right to amend a generosity you've extended. Do this as soon as you see signs that someone can't or won't observe your appropriate limits.

"Maddie, when I said your friends could call my number till you get your own phone, I didn't realize your friends would be calling you after midnight. I have to withdraw my offer."

"Sun Li, how did I know he would call then? Don't punish me for what Cal did."

"I'm just taking care of myself here. I would never have offered if I'd known your friends would be calling so late."

"I told him not to do that. He does it anyway."

"Well, if he doesn't respect your request, he sure isn't going to respect mine."

"We could put your phone in my room. Then it wouldn't bother you."

"No, it's my phone. I want it in my room. I'm turning off the ringer when I go to sleep."

You also have the right to withdraw a courtesy if it turns out not to be working well for you—even if the other person is responding with respect and regard.

"Hawk, I know I said you could use my computer, but it just isn't working for me. You aren't doing anything wrong. You've paid attention to everything I've asked of you. I didn't realize when I offered it that I'd feel the way I do. My whole life is on that computer. Even though you're my best friend, I feel like someone is walking into my brain when you use it."

"I'm really hurt, Donna. I did everything you asked."

"I know you did, Hawk. This isn't about you. It's about me. I offered more than I could afford to, and I just didn't realize it until afterwards."

"This bums me out. Now I'll have to go to Kinko's to do my letters."

"I know. I'm sorry."

Should Donna pay for Hawk to use the computer at Kinko's? No. If Donna had never offered, Hawk still would have had to find a computer somewhere else.

Should Donna investigate the library and see if Hawk could use that computer for free? No, it's up to Hawk to discover his options. Donna is not now obligated to do something extra for Hawk just because she found out she couldn't follow through with her offer.

Hawk is not in any worse situation as a result of Donna's decision. He has already benefited from the use of the computer he's had up to this point. Hopefully, when he gets past his initial irritation, he'll remember that he did receive a gift from Donna, and that Donna is due some gratitude.

WHAT IF?

If you said you'll take care of your friend's dog while she's on vacation, and you have a fight with her right before she leaves, what is appropriate?

1. Make yourself do it even though your heart isn't in it.
2. Realize that the dog is innocent and deserves good care.
3. Blow off the friend and the dog.
4. Tell her that you can't take care of Barks, even though she leaves on her flight at 5 A.M. the next morning.

The correct response is 2. It's not fair to make the dog a victim of your human disagreement. Nor is it fair to your friend (even if she's now an ex-friend) to renege on a commitment you made in good faith when a close deadline is involved.

If you can't stomach caring for her pet, you can find someone else to do it or contribute some cash for a kennel, if your friend has time to make other arrangements.

GOOD POSSESSION BOUNDARIES

- Protect the things you cherish.
- Don't dispose of items that carry meaning for you, even when pressured to do so by a loved one.
- Set limits for items that are too personal to be lent to others.
- Set limits when you see that another person has a different sense of what is appropriate than you do.
- Withdraw an offer if it turns out not to feel right to you.

- When another person reveals that they will exploit your generosity, be careful not to offer them too much.
- Define how you want your possessions treated. If someone can't or won't respect your requests, don't give them further access to those possessions.
- If your relationship with someone changes, it's okay to withdraw offers that no longer fit the altered relationship. However, if the other person is depending on your offer and withdrawal will create a hardship for them, either find another way to fulfill the terms of your offer or give the person compensation.

Chapter 18

PARENT BOUNDARIES

After her husband died, Maidie was lonely and scared, so she had her son sleep in the same bed with her. She turned to him in sorrow, seeking comfort. She clung to him and sobbed through the days and nights of her emptiness.

Her son was six years old. He was too young for this burden. He did not have the maturity to handle such an intense, extended emotion. He was also too young to be able to say no to her exploitation.

Though Maidie's need and pain are completely understandable, it was still not okay for her to use her child this way. Children can't say no to the will of adults. This is why they must be protected from situations that require more than they have the resources to handle.

The 1998 film *Life Is Beautiful* captured many hearts and received several awards. It demonstrates one parent's extraordinary efforts to protect his son from an unfathomable situation. Such a high standard of fathering gives the rest of us something to shoot for.

We adults get desperate and lonely and frightened, but we

do have options and resources. In every community, someone is available to help. We are the adults. We can make choices.

Children have limited resources and even more limited choices. Their perspective does not reach beyond their families. The younger they are, the less their capacity to realize that they can say no, that they can ask for help, or that their parent's behavior is wrong.

Parents draw a circle in the sand with their behavior. Everything within the circle is seen as normal to a child. Everything on the outside is seen as abnormal. Children become imprinted with this distinction, and it determines their view of the world, their beliefs about relationships, and their sense of themselves.

If the circle contains respect for differences, kindness, and love, children become adults with the ability to create their own circle of love and tolerance. If the circle contains anger, threat, abuse, or disregard, children grow up hating themselves, everyone else, or both. When such children reach adulthood, they will find kindness and generosity abnormal, possibly even suspicious.

A circle containing neglect, exploitation, control, criticism, and estrangement will sprout a lonely child who does not know how to belong, feels undeserving and unfulfilled, and has difficulty connecting with others. This child could become an adult who finds tolerance abnormal.

Children are so steeped in the culture of their family that once they become adults, it is difficult and wrenching for them to wash themselves of it. As a result, they then raise their own kids in a similar culture. Thus any distortions tend to be passed down through the generations.

STOP THE BUCK

Here is where therapy shines. It can be the fastest, most effective way to dismantle the dysfunction that spirals from one generation to the next. Adults who cleanse themselves of their childhood programming do a much better job raising their own children. They can create a new family culture—one that promotes joy and happiness for their kids.

Since children can't know what is normal and what is not, it's up to the adults in a family to discipline themselves to stay within healthy limits and to turn to other adults to have their emotional and physical needs met.

BOUNDARIES WITH CHILDREN, PART I

1. Do not exploit children.
2. Do not turn to them with your complex adult issues, needs, or feelings.
3. Do not seek physical comfort from them by making them sleep with you for an extended period.
4. Do not seek any manner of sexual gratification from them.
5. Do not touch them sexually. Do not use their bodies in any way for your sexual relief.
6. Do not look at them sexually.
7. Do not make sexual comments to them.
8. Do not comment about other people in a sexual way in front of them.
9. Do not expose them to sexual materials, publications, or devices.

APPROPRIATE DEGREES OF RESPONSIBILITY

Yolanda Race had wanted a dog ever since she was a pup herself. Finally, the improbable happened; when she was eleven, her mother relented. Yolanda could have a dog, but she'd have to be totally responsible for it.

Yolanda took good care of Woofer. However, the county required that all dogs be licensed and have innoculations. The vet's bill came to $64.

Mrs. Race refused to pay it. From the start she had told Yolanda she would have to be responsible for her pet. She insisted that bill was Yolanda's problem.

Yolanda didn't get an allowance and wasn't old enough to baby-sit. She had no way to make money. The bill went unpaid and went into collections. The family received notice to go to court.

In court, Mrs. Race explained to the judge that the bill was Yolanda's responsibility. He looked at the little, frail-looking girl standing before him, brought down the gavel, and declared that the parents would have to pay the bill.

Mrs. Race was so upset that, as punishment, she left Yolanda in downtown Seattle to find her own way home.

What is true about this situation?

1. Yolanda was irresponsible for not paying the bill.
2. Yolanda was charged with a responsibility she had no way to fulfill.
3. It's an appropriate punishment to endanger a child.

The obvious answer here is 2.

Of course we shouldn't abandon children to dangerous situations, even if we are overwhelmed, or mad at them, or dealing with big problems of our own. But the point of this (sadly) true story is that Yolanda was given a responsibility she could not meet. A quick way to teach children that they are inadequate is to give them jobs they can't possibly handle.

Children who are charged with such jobs as making their parents happy, keeping a parent safe, solving a parent's difficulties in the world, giving a parent a reason to stay alive, or fulfilling a parent's dreams are set up to fail.

These are impossible tasks. No one can make another person happy. We each have to find our own reasons to stay alive. We are charged with fulfilling our own dreams.

Yet children absorb and accept whatever job expectations they are given, even if they are unspoken, and then unconsciously try to fulfill them—sometimes their whole lives long. Since they can't possibly succeed, they can also—for a lifetime—believe that they aren't up to snuff.

Even when these kids grow up, they continue to carry the same roles, and rarely do they realize on a conscious level that they can quit. They may feel compelled to move far away from their parents or to transfer all their attention to their own adult households, but the chances are they will continue to try doing the same job for the new people in their lives. We can be turned inside out a long, long time when we've been trained to be too responsible as small children.

EMOTIONAL NEGLECT

Few creatures can thrive with just food, water, and shelter. Fish school, birds flock, animals herd—even some insects behave cooperatively. Lizards live independently, but most other creatures need contact with their own kind.

Children too need more than food, water, and shelter. They need physical and emotional safety, safe touch, limits, consistency, clear communication, instruction, and routine contact.

Emotional neglect occurs when parents are so involved in their adult pursuits that their children get short shrift. When children are pushed aside, made to wait an eternity to have time with a parent, or forced to endure broken promises because of the endless work demands of their parents, they learn that they are less important than achievement, money, or material gain. Emotional neglect ultimately causes great damage to the child's self-esteem and to their ability to be in a relationship.

Don't be a lizard. Talk to your children. Listen to them. Play with them. Construct events and activities that you can share with them. Teach them how the world works. Demonstrate honest, ethical behavior. Show how to handle anger in a healthy way. Practice negotiation with them. Teach them to express feelings, to grieve, to communicate.

Prepare them for their emancipation by (when they are old enough) showing them how to handle money, maintain a car, thank others for gifts, cook healthy food, take care of clothing, exercise, respond to invitations, initiate contact with others, and all the other skills that adults need to enjoy life.

BOUNDARIES WITH CHILDREN, PART II

1. Attend to their emotional, psychological, physical, and spiritual needs.
2. Teach them love, acceptance, and tolerance.

3. Help them belong, both within the family and with other groups they enter.

4. Teach them to handle feelings, resolve conflict, and ne-gotiate.

5. Prepare them for adulthood.

Chapter 19

SPIRITUAL BOUNDARIES

Throughout human history, the apostles of purity, those who have claimed to possess a total explanation, have wrought havoc among mere mixed-up human beings.

—SALMAN RUSHDIE

Beckah lost her parents in an auto accident and was sent at twelve years of age to live with her aunt. Aunt Van was tediously religious and gleamed with righteousness. She was one of those rare humans who follows even the minor rules. She dusted the lintels of the doorways. She filled out her taxes on January 5. She packed for a trip four weeks in advance (and unpacked minutes after arriving home).

Beckah's first week with her aunt extended the child's shock. She sat on a couch and was shooed to a plastic-covered chair. She reached for a second helping of green beans and was lectured on gluttony. At night she shivered in her hard bed, afraid to ask for another blanket. She came home from school to find that her Nancy Drew mysteries were missing. A hesitant question to Aunt Van produced a storm of words about the secular and depraved popular culture. Beckah got the message that studying anything but holy books was frowned on by God.

Her aunt read from the Scriptures daily and prayed extensively and loudly about Beckah's shortcomings. Aunt Van was tactlessly expressive that God's judgment had culled her sister, Beckah's mother, from earthly life because of her great sin in marrying outside the faith. To the flinty religiosity of her aunt, Beckah added a God who stole loving parents, and decided she could do without a religion that fanned pain.

It is hard for children to separate a view of God from the distortions of some of His followers. When children grow up in households full of judgment and harsh piety, when they are hit over the head with the name of God, when they are steeped in messages that turn them against their positive instincts and interests, when they are taught to hate their bodies and their humanness, barricades are placed across the path to God.

Being in contact with your own spiritual nature and learning to access your connection with God are essential aspects of being fully human. Any person or group that attempts to block these connections commits a violation of spiritual boundaries.

If you find yourself stifled by your religion, examine what is happening. Is your religious community leading you closer to God, improving your relationship with the most High, enhancing your communion with others, including nonbelievers? If not, your particular religious group could be subtly violating your spiritual boundaries.

A relationship with God is life-giving. It opens and expands consciousness and perception. We learn that certain behaviors can harm this holy relationship, not because God abandons us, but because when we make certain mistakes, we want to turn away from God.

True spirituality forces us to find the incredibly wobbly middle ground between the passions of humanness and the boundaries that hold us in a place of respecting and honoring, not only God, but His entire creation, including the earth and all its creatures.

"The Lord laid it on my heart that you are to donate your money to the church and move to Gustavus."

"The Lord visited me in a dream and He said you are to be my wife."

"My religion is the only true religion."

What is the problem with statements like these?

1. The Lord's name is being used to control another person.

2. Someone is placing himself in a position of spiritual superiority over another.

3. The Lord's boundary is being violated.

All of the above statements are true. The Creator is the supreme respecter of boundaries, presenting us with revelations, models, and clear pathways to seek Him out; but He never, never violates volition. Of all the beings in the universe, the Supreme Being is the one with the utmost power to make us do things His way. And He never uses it. He gave us free will and, by God, He sticks to it, come hell or high water.

I know I get irritated when someone misrepresents me. I wonder how the Holy One feels about being used this way. He did mention He didn't like his name being taken in vain. Perhaps this qualifies. At any rate, a lot of harm has been done in the name of God—wars fought, people sacrificed, women and races subjugated, politics and government influenced.

We occasionally run into people who have all the answers, who believe they have an inside track to the mind of God. I've had people come to my door to tell me of their take on God. I think it takes great courage to walk through strange neighborhoods and risk the gamut of responses from householders. I've invited in some of these apostles and what has struck me each time is how impossible it is to truly converse about God with these brave people.

Since we both hold God in our hearts, it would seem that we could share the joy of our respective relationships. But I've found that my attempts at a real conversation run into an inflexible wall. Another agenda is behind the scenes. Their interest is in convincing me that their group is the only one with the correct path to God.

I was raised in a religious environment that was strong on the love relationship with God and others and weak in doctrine. Still, I got the clear message that Christianity was the only path that didn't dead-end before heaven's gate.

I traveled in Italy with a group of spiritual seekers that was using unconventional ways of connecting with Spirit, such as dance and drawing and dreaming, and borrowing practices from other religions beside Christianity. I occasionally worried that I'd strayed beyond the interstate and was on a goat path to nowhere, definitely beyond the margins of my childhood religion.

We entered a doma in Sicily, a cathedral built on the foundations and using the pillars of a temple to Apollo, which itself had been built on the site of worship of a mother goddess. It had been a mecca for spiritual seekers for four millennia. I went over to a pillar and lay my forehead against it and instantly was transported into a vision.

I saw golden columns, like pillars of light that stretched from Earth to the spiritual realm and these were made of the prayers and meditations of all the people turning to God. Prayers were traveling like beams of golden sunshine and as they connected with the Almighty the answers came vibrating back in similar golden pathways. This pulsing of prayers and responses created shining cables all over the world.

I understood with a largeness beyond words that it wasn't doctrine or sect that mattered but the devoutness of the believer. Anyone truly seeking after God, regardless of the religious form it took, was participating in this brilliant synergy.

It's these occasional gifts from the Almighty that reveal to me how limited is our earthly perspective, how much bigger God is than we can wrap our minds around. We take a little piece and try to make sense of it and before long we have a religion full of rules and suppositions that can be far from God's true nature and intent.

Humans sometimes try to use the name of God to control others. They sometimes try to force their concepts about God onto others. This is a violation of the receiver's spiritual boundaries. God has already demonstrated God's way of doing things.

The Creator never forces spirituality or goodness on anyone. He may offer you so many opportunities you'd have to be blind to miss the invitation, but you are never forced to accept any of them. If you ask, however obliquely, God's Spirit will be there in a flash, but you have to ask.

The Bible is full of examples of the way God works. When religious people went off the deep end, God found creative ways to correct them. Saul (Paul) was struck blind with the message to lay off the first Christians, Peter was told to relax about dietary restrictions, and David was told not to grab women. Jesus, who had an inside line, never forced anyone to think His way. He did get irritated with the pharisees for abusing their position of leadership, and we've been warned that abuse of religious leadership does not set well with the Heavenly Consciousness.

God never forced a prophet or potential saint to take the holy path. God did send an occasional engraved invitation. Mary was asked if she wanted to bear God's child, and Joseph was told to support her even if things looked dicey. Noah was told to take up carpentry. Samuel was told to surrender to God. Each person could have said no.

Notice that none of these folks were told to use their spiritual connection to coerce anybody else. Moses did set the first boundaries (after Yahweh drew a line around the tree in Eden), but even then he didn't try forcing people to follow them. Instead, he warned of the consequences, and ever since then we've been, one at a time, learning over and over the consequences of ignoring God's boundaries.

We humans are each called to work out our own connection with God. It's a relationship, one to one, between each of us and God—a direct line. We are given, in each generation, wise guides and outstanding examples of how to do so, but the choices and the actions must be our own.

So, what can you do when someone presumes to be God's personal ambassador, sent to set you straight? (I'm of course not talking about a priest, minister, rabbi, or religious teacher from whom you've sought guidance.) Set a boundary that establishes your own separate spiritual territory.

"Thanks for your thoughts. I'll turn to God myself on this matter."

"God told me you should mind your own business. Just kidding."

"Is His message still on your answering machine? I'd like to hear it myself."

"What did God tell you you should do about *your* life?"

"That's strange, God's message to me was quite different."

"I'm sure you didn't mean to violate my spiritual boundaries, but now that you have, please don't give me such messages again. I have my own strong relationship with the Creator. It gives me much joy and guidance. For you to try to step between us—God and me—is disrespectful of both of us. If you have judgments about my spirituality, remember that God said not to judge, lest He judge you."

Chapter 20

TIDINESS BOUNDARIES

Tidiness, or the lack of it, creates all sorts of issues for people. What is the appropriate range for tidiness in a home? How quickly should untidiness be responded to? How does a guest respect the tidiness boundaries of a host? Does a boss have a say over an employee's tidiness? Does an employee have a say over a boss's tidiness?

As I pile up more years of working with clients, I've come to believe that tidiness is not a superficial issue about good housekeeping, but an external expression of a variety of important, heartfelt internal processes. The degree of one's tidiness can directly relate to their energy, health, emotional clarity, cultural values, priorities, upbringing, scarcity, fear, busyness, compulsiveness, perfectionism, and sense of home.

Cultures vary in their perception of what constitutes untidiness and clutter. When I moved to Seattle, I rented a room for six months in the home of a family from China. Each room was perfectly neat at all times. Furnishings were spare and carefully placed. Two family members, however, aspired to be as American as possible. These two people had acquired a great many more items than the others, and their rooms were much more cluttered.

Of course, tidiness is not entirely a function of the number of items in a room. I've seen crowded rooms that were exquisitely organized, and stark rooms that felt filthy because crumbs and crusted dishes littered all the surfaces. Nevertheless, when the volume of items overwhelms the space in which they are kept, a certain critical point gets passed, and chaos results.

Is there an American standard of tidiness? I'm amused by a straw poll I've been taking for years. In nearly every neighborhood, there is one house in perfect order. Its paint is fresh; vehicles are lined up or put away; the grass is regularly mowed; flower beds are primly ordered. Also in nearly every neighborhood, there is at least one house in disarray. The grass is shaggy; trash cans lie on their sides; and all sorts of flotsam and jetsam litter the property.

I've also noticed that, with rare exceptions, people will apologize for the state of their homes, no matter how neat their homes actually are. I've concluded that, as a rule, we believe we should be tidier than we are, that most ordinary Americans believe they are falling short in their neatness duties.

Tidiness has advantages. We can find things. For the amount of time it takes to maintain tidiness, we are paid back in time that isn't needed to hunt for things.

The Asian art of feng shui is all about arranging space to enhance health and ease. As I've applied these principles, I've discovered that I do increase the energy of a room when it is tidy and well arranged.

We each fall somewhere on a continuum between a home

that is dangerously cluttered and one that is surgically sterile. If you live alone, a wide swath on the continuum is acceptable. A boundary is crossed only if your health or comfortable living is threatened, or if your tidiness (or lack of it) is actually a defense against some inner fear.

For example, if you are so busy tidying and cleaning that you miss out on living a rich, varied life, you've violated your own boundary. Such rampant tidying could be an effort to create a feeling of control in a chaotic world—an understandable reaction, perhaps, but costly in terms of quality of life.

At the other end of the scale, severe clutter can crowd people out. Some folks might avoid a house that could double as a news archive, that offers no clean place to sit, or that reeks with unpleasant odors.

The integrity of your home life becomes compromised when your issues with cleaning interfere with your ability to keep your environment the way you'd really like it. If something inside you is violating the way you'd like to live, do you know what is behind this interference? Working with the internal issue in a therapeutic way, or with a professional clutter coach, can help.

IT TAKES TWO TO TANGLE

The tidiness issue heats up considerably when two people live together. You've heard of the law of gravity, and you know instinctively of the law of the left sock (the sock that's abandoned when its mate escapes through the dryer vent and hops merrily to Sock Camp).

Now let me introduce you to a nearly inviolable law I've discovered, the Law of Heterotidiality. This law ordains that a very tidy person always marries one who tends to clutter. Survival of the species is thus promoted by keeping a couple's home balanced between the extremes of drowning in debris and ringing with cries of, "Oh no, I threw that out and now I need it!"

Li, who is energized by tidiness and loves order, can be perpetually irritated by Fan, who leaves tools where they were last used. Fan's perspective is that being a good parent, doing a good job, or simply living a full life matters more than a few tumbling piles. Li needs for things to be tidy in order to have energy for the kids or for Fan, and thus is thwarted by clutter. Fan sees Li's standard of neatness as arbitrary and feels confined by it.

I've had a fair sprinkling of clients who were neglected as children, not by an absent or drinking mom, but by one who was driven to keep things tidy. These mothers were so devoted to keeping their households showroom perfect that they didn't see their children's lonely eyes. Taught by painful experience that the house was more important than they were, these kids couldn't find their own place in either the house or their mother's heart.

Not surprisingly, these adult children of compulsive tidiers have difficulty keeping their own homes in order. Another consequence is that many of them live alone and feel doomed to be alone in the world. Some essential connections got missed while mom was polishing the furniture.

So what *are* appropriate boundaries around tidiness?

First, respect the needs of each member of the household regarding their own possessions and their own private space. If Shanna keeps her tools in perfect order, put them back when you borrow them. If Harold feels violated when you move things on his desk, leave his desk alone.

Second, if at all possible, create an inviolable space for each member of the household—a room, a closet, an alcove that can be screened, a corner where each person can be cluttered or tidy to their heart's content. Keep out of their spaces and leave their things alone. Close the door or pull a curtain if company is coming.

Third, when you are a guest in someone's home, model your tidiness parameters according to what you see your host doing. If they neaten the room at the end of the day, don't leave your socks in the living room. If they carry plates to the sink, do the same.

If you are tidier than your host, create the order you need in your own area, and stop there. Always ask permission be fore straightening or cleaning a host's home. It is a gross boundary violation, no matter what your motive, to clean out someone else's closet or organize their drawers—unless of course you have first gotten their express and enthusiastic permission.

At work, negotiate tidiness boundaries that promote your own productivity. If your boss insists on a neat desk, but a barren work surface shuts you out of the creative part of your brain, tell your boss why you need to work differently. If you need neatness to have a clear head, explain why dumping out a drawer on your desk will set you back for a couple of hours. (Obviously, a monstrously untidy place of business will also turn away clients. On the other hand, stalking a client with a dust mop sends a forbidding message.)

An appropriate tidiness boundary is one that protects the integrity of the environment and *the integrity of the people who use it.* Tidiness boundaries also exclude any extreme that violates the space of others, interferes with anyone's quality of life, threatens anyone's health, or gets in the way of intimacy.

My sister serves as a good model here. Her house is always comfortable. It's easy to find room to play a game, have a conversation, or share a meal. There are places to sit and room to move, and the house is clean enough to feel healthy. Yet when someone visits, she sits down and attends to them. She doesn't track them with a vacuum cleaner or wait till she's completed twenty chores before she talks to them. Her whole home is designed and maintained according to two priorities: living comfortably and having space to connect.

Chapter 21

DRESS AND APPEARANCE BOUNDARIES

It is an interesting question how far men would retain their relative
rank if they were divested of their clothes.

—THOREAU

Our appearance and attire are the first signals we send to people. By our attire we reveal who we are, what we care about,
and in some cases what we are busy doing at the moment.

Costume has always been a way to announce tribal connection. This is as true now for operagoers in Manhattan and
rad teenagers at the mall as it was thousands of years ago
when humans drew patterns on their animal-skin garments.

Clothing and appearance can proclaim a boundary or the
lack of one. Clothing can be a neon sign that states your position in the world and how you expect to be treated. We can
also use clothing as a defense, deliberately dressing in a way
that shuts certain people out or scares them off.

On the other hand, clothing can invite some people too
close. An outfit that is too skimpy or suggestive may broad-

cast that a boundary is missing, and could send an engraved invitation to someone with sexual exploitation on their agenda.

What are good boundaries of dress? Where are the appropriate limits that balance the needs of the culture with individual expression? How much of a fight should there be between parents and adolescent children about clothing?

ADOLESCENT FASHION, AN OXYMORON?

Each new adolescent generation is remarkably creative in finding styles that will cause elders to gnash their teeth. Adults feel instinctively that their own culture is being rejected, and the friction thus created gives emancipating adolescents a separate part of the pond in which to finish developing and become individual.

These days the dangers in that separate place seem greater than they used to be. This gives the overseers of teenagers a more complicated responsibility. We have to let kids find their own way, but we don't want them to die, or destroy their brains or bodies, as they make the transition.

Yelling at children, making derogatory comments, does not win them to your point of view. A teenage girl will probably rebel against a father who calls her a slut, and dress even more provocatively. A son won't want to comply with a mother who says he looks stupid with jeans hanging around his knees. The anger that lies beneath such comments will only promote further estrangement and contempt.

Remember that teenagers are sensitive and vulnerable and want to be accepted by the teenage clan. Find ways to compromise. When you want your child to mix with members of your own culture, ask for (and, sometimes, even insist on) compliance with your idea of appropriate dress. But when they're with their peers, let them dress more or less as they please.

I remember a dear thing my grandmother did when I was a teenager. I went to a party at our church, peeked through the door, and saw that all the girls were wearing flats. I was wearing high heels. I backed away, went to the phone, called home, and asked my grandmother to bring me flat-heeled shoes.

Some other parent might have reacted with a disparaging comment. "For heaven's sake, it's not that important. Grow up. It's not a big deal for you to be wearing different shoes." But I was fortunate. My grandmother understood that I ached to be accepted and that I would rather miss the party than stand out as different. She brought the shoes immediately, even though we lived a few miles away, and I waited in the foyer until she drove up. With the right shoes I could enter the party and enjoy it without being self-conscious.

ADULT FASHION

The fastest way to enter into a culture is to adopt its fashion. If you wear clothing that is shockingly different from the group you wish to join, you will be making a statement of individuality, but you will not be taken all the way in until you are known. We set up extra miles of proving ourselves when we dress quite differently from the others in our milieu.

I've never seen a surgeon or a judge with obvious multiple body piercings. A bikini would get a lot of attention at a church Christmas concert in Montana. A three-piece suit in Hawaii looks confining and uncomfortable.

If you dress quite differently from the norm in your work-place, area, or community, you are making a statement. Is this a statement you want to make? Do you want to separate yourself in that setting? (Maybe you do. That's fine, so long as you accept the consequences of that decision.)

In a business environment, clothing that is too casual or sexual can prevent promotion. At a job interview, an appearance that sets you apart can make interviewers wary. Unusual dress in a retail setting might draw one group of customers and warn off another. Be careful not to push away the ones who would buy your product.

Clothing and presentation can be vehicles that carry you in or keep you out. Take time now and then to think about the messages you are sending in the various settings in which you live and work. Are those messages congruent with the results you want to have?

ACCEPTING DIFFERENCES

Twenty years ago, when I was visiting my grandmother in a nursing home, all the women wore what we called house dresses. My grandmother never wore a pair of trousers or jeans her entire life. I remember trying to picture those elders in jeans and thinking it hilarious. Now everyone I know, regardless of age, wears jeans. It's more common to see denims on a grandmother than on a toddler.

As each generation ages, it brings a new wave of fashion into the next higher age bracket. The generation that wore jeans in the sixties carried jeans into workplaces and retirement communities. The generation that wore T-shirts as teenagers carried that style into adulthood. Today, T-shirts can be accessorized and are often made from fine fabrics.

Before you judge another's attire, consider cultural and regional differences. For my first Thanksgiving in the Northwest, I dressed for dinner as we did in the South. Mine was the only long skirt among the jeans. I last wore a pair of heels six years ago, at a friend's wedding. I had to go out and buy them, because I no longer owned high-heeled shoes.

It's been said that Northwest fashion is an oxymoron, like fresh frozen jumbo shrimp. The uniform of the Northwest is casual, but it suits me (and apparently many others who place comfort and flexibility over style).

Each region has its own parameters of what constitutes propriety. In the South and Midwest, certain social groups have strict customs about dress. Shoes and purse must match. No white shoes between Labor Day and Memorial Day. In parts of Appalachia, a mark of respect is donning a clean apron when a guest arrives.

When you are welcoming a visitor from another region, remember that a style that looks eccentric to you may be reflecting the norm of that person's home territory. You may appear just as surprising to them.

People react instinctively (and often negatively) to dress that is eccentric to their place, culture, or generation. We are wise to take that into account when we seek to belong. On the other hand, when we already do belong, and we're in the position of receiving a newcomer, we can afford to regard eccentricity with more latitude. We can accept the differences we notice, trading judgment and criticism for the fresh interest that can be revealed by another's individuality.

FROZEN BY FASHION

The appearance issue becomes a problem when it interferes with living. Changing outfits six times because we want to make a good impression on a first date is understandable, but missing the party because we feel unattractive is a more serious situation.

Any time we deprive ourselves of enjoying an experience, taking a trip, or risking a new venture because we judge ourselves unattractive or physically unacceptable in some way, we are being controlled too much by image. If we have a narrow view of our appearance and are self-conscious about not being Hollywood perfect, we may shy from a contact or smother our natural expressiveness and give an incorrect message that derails a potentially valuable relationship.

It's not your appearance, but the attitudes you have about it, that affect someone's response to you. Clara Oaks felt shy about her weight. She carried extra pounds around a beautiful warm heart and a thoughtful approach to life. She was a wonderful friend. When she met someone new, male or female, she was certain they were seeing only her body size. She held herself back. She revealed very little of herself and carried an air of stiffness. She telegraphed the message, "Stay away."

Most people didn't try to get closer. She believed that was because of her size, but it was her attitude about her size that pushed them away.

If you hold back because you're having a bad hair day or because your outfit is ten years old or because your shoes are scuffed, the other person will sense the energy, but is likely to misinterpret the reason. You'll get the distance you expected, but not because of your appearance. They'll take the message as being about them or as a sign of your coolness toward them, and that message is what will make them back off.

The truth is, most other people don't dwell on how we look. When we see someone for the first time, their appearance registers—primarily so we can identify them—and then we soon see further inside that person. If someone judges and dismisses you because of what's on the outside, you've lost nothing. Such a superficial person isn't worthy of you.

Live your full life. Don't miss a party because of a pimple. Don't keep yourself from a gala because you can't afford a new outfit. The important thing about life is experiencing all the rich variety of goodness that is offered.

Chapter 22

Boundaries for Illness and Chronic Conditions

Illness

Nora came down with a bad case of pneumonia that lasted for weeks. Already situated in an assisted living retirement home, she got good care. But she was bedridden, and while she was sick she was transferred into the hospital wing.

A friend, also living in the same home but mobile and in a self-contained apartment, called her one morning and said she'd come down that evening so they could watch *60 Minutes* together.

Nora looked forward to the visit. When she felt a little stronger that day, she moved the chair so it would be better placed for her friend's viewing. She prepared herself for her friend's arrival, propping herself up in bed, getting the correct TV station, and mustering her energy for the occasion.

60 Minutes started, and Nora realized she'd seen it, but for her friend's sake, she kept that station on, rather than switching to another program she would have preferred.

She waited through the entire program.

An hour and a half late, her friend showed up. "What would you like to do?" she said.

Nora didn't know how to respond. She had geared her energy for the previous hour and now she was tired again. The visit had already taken more from her than it had given.

Healing takes a lot of energy. When a person is battling a disease or recovering from surgery, they have limited resources for handling social situations. When they are expecting you to visit within a certain time period, they garner their energy for that time. If you miss that period, they will have two strikes against them. Their energy will be on the wane, plus they'll be angry or disappointed that you didn't follow through, and that eats up still more energy. Furthermore, they are in a vulnerable situation, so they'll feel reluctant to express their anger and disappointment. That only gives them one more thing to handle.

We may sometimes think that since someone who is ill is just lying there all day, it doesn't matter when we show up. But to a person who is bedridden and dependent, time is very important. It passes too slowly, especially if they are waiting for the joy and interest your visit will bring. Each minute you are late, they are watching the clock and losing a minute of energy. If you are very late—or, worse, miss the time period entirely—they may not be able to recover the energy they spent in feeling unimportant or abandoned while they waited.

When a person is dependent, little things matter a lot. So follow through if you make a promise, because any promise you make will be taken seriously.

If you are an hour late and the person says, "I'm just glad you came," they are being gracious. Don't take it at face value. Ask, "Is it hard on you if I'm late? Would you feel better if I gave you a general window of time when I might visit rather than a specific time?"

CHRONIC PHYSICAL ILLNESS

Janet had several autoimmune diseases that dictated the parameters of her life. Her energy would ebb and flow like a tidal river, except that she had no chart to tell her when a surge would start or when she'd be felled by bottomless fatigue.

Despite this, she managed to work part-time, attend church, keep an apartment, and carry out the responsibilities of daily living. However, she did this only through meticulous management of her internal resources.

Her activities were carefully sprinkled throughout the week. If she wanted to go to the church picnic, she'd have to skip the service itself. She couldn't just run out to the store; she'd combine trips so that walking to the car and walking to the store served more than one purpose. Her entire life was organized around the wise budgeting of her energy.

Now and then she would grieve for the activities she'd have to sacrifice in order to do the ones she wanted or needed most. At times her life seemed harder because she had no partner to ease the burden or share the chores and decisions.

Now and then new friends would enter the picture. At first, they would be a great boon. They'd be full of willingness to help and energetically tromp up and down the stairs to her apartment. By transporting her and assisting her, she'd be able to do more. She loved the expanded possibilities when people helped her.

But eventually many of these friends would burn out—having given too much—and would go away. When she would hesitate in making a decision, carefully weighing her capacity for an activity, they would sometimes view it as a manipulation. Because she would seem normal much of the time—the result of her careful and methodical management of her personal energy—some of her friends came to believe that she could overcome her disability with the right attitude, if only she'd try.

THE GREAT DIVIDE

We in the United States live at a pace that constantly demands optimum performance of our bodies (and our tools, our employees, our cars, computers, children, and mates). We get impatient when our cell phones don't connect to a tower immediately. We drum our fingers if the computer needs an extra second to think.

We have no space for illness, fatigue, or aging. Many of us treat our bodies like machines, demanding endless resilience of ever-diminishing resources. No wonder the incidence of chronic and autoimmune diseases is rising at an alarming rate.

When people become ill, they cross the great divide to the ranks of the infirm. Meanwhile, the healthy people rush on. There's a way healthy people separate themselves from those with illness.

Partly this is just the nature of living. While we are alive, we want all the involvement that living can provide. But I wonder if something else—a denial or fear of the prospect of illness—enhances the separation.

Usually people with autoimmune and chronic diseases want very much to participate in whatever life they can manage. Most don't want to be seen as separate or different, and many find it difficult to ask for the concessions that would make participation easier for them. If everyone is standing, it can be hard to ask for a chair.

Janet loved attending her prayer group, but sometimes a member's house would be so far away that she couldn't muster the energy to drive there. She missed meetings now and then because of this. She wanted so much not to be seen as different, but one day, as hard as it was, she forced herself to say that she wanted to go but didn't think she could manage the drive.

Because she did marshal the courage to speak, the entire prayer group suddenly caught on to her dilemma. They had a wonderful conversation in which Janet shared her enjoyment of the group and the difficulty she faced when she didn't have the energy to drive herself to meetings. She even talked about how hard it was to have needs that were different from everyone else's.

Understanding opened up, and the group volunteered to take turns picking her up so that she could always go, no matter where the meeting was held. She felt included, wanted, and warmly supported. Over time, the group realized that the care and patience that Janet's illness had taught her often held wisdom for them.

We have each gained wisdom by walking our unique path. Everyone has something to offer. By shunning the chronically ill, we deprive ourselves of perspectives that can slow us down and inform us.

THE DILEMMA OF THE BEDRIDDEN

The minute her grandkids came through the door, Elsie bombarded them with a long list of things she needed them to do.

"Mona, take my nighties to be washed. I'm out of powder. Bring me some books next time. Change the channel on the TV, Ted. Move my phone—the maid put it out of reach."

Ted and Mona sometimes felt invisible to her, as if they were mere servants, not her treasured offspring. They felt unimportant and, as a result, didn't visit Elsie very often.

A bedridden person is completely dependent on the legs and arms of anyone who comes through the door. As a result, they can easily get in the habit of greeting relatives with a list of their needs, out of fear that if they don't, they'll end up lying there waiting for another day, week, or month before someone can respond to them.

If you are healthy, appreciate that a bedridden person must always wait to have any needs met. This is very hard. If they can write, encourage them to keep a running list of things they need. If they are alert, get them a little tape recorder and teach them how to record their needs as they come up.

Whenever you visit them, let them know right away how long you'll be there. If they know they'll have plenty of time with you, they won't feel they have to get all their requests out in the first five minutes. It can also help if, when you first arrive, you reassure them that you'll pay attention to their list.

Make physical contact to help them come out of their awful isolation. Hold their hands, brush their hair, touch their arm (unless, of course, any of this is painful). Touch will help them relax and be more present.

BOUNDARIES WITH PEOPLE WHO ARE BEDRIDDEN

- If you see a way a kindness can benefit them, offer it.
- When you first arrive, always say how long you'll be there. Stick to this commitment.

- Keep the promises you make. If you say you'll visit again in two weeks, do so.
- Offer to listen to their experiences. Being understood can give them energy and fortify them for the next week of living. Let them talk about what they go through, how they view the staff, who their favorite caregiver is, and so on.
- Take care to give only what you can afford to give. Be careful not to extend yourself so far that you'll resent it.
- Observe your own (often automatic) judgments and criticisms of the person. Try to spot any unfair or automatic assumptions. Do your best not to act on assumptions, but to respond to the living, breathing, unique person before you.

KEEPING GOOD BOUNDARIES IF YOU HAVE A CHRONIC ILLNESS

- Greet your visitors before getting into a discussion about what they can provide and how they can help you.
- When a visitor first arrives, ask them how long they plan to stay so that you can pace yourself for their visit.
- Ask directly for what you need or want. Remember, you are the world's leading expert on your situation. You may have to explain exactly what you need to people unfamiliar with your illness.
- Express your appreciation for what people offer you. If someone gives you time, a treat, or help, this is a gift. Thank them.
- Remember, anyone who serves you does so out of choice. You are not entitled to their help. You are fortunate that others will give you the help you need.

- Do not manipulate others to get what you need. People pick up the energy of manipulation, and then begin setting up defenses against you.
- Keep a running list of the things you need on a piece of paper or cassette tape.
- It will expand your world to find out about the lives and activities of your visitors. Ask them what they are involved in and what matters to them.

CHRONIC EMOTIONAL DISORDERS

Before Kevin married Marra, she explained that she had suffered for most of her life from severe mood swings that were finally diagnosed as bipolar disorder and were now successfully treated by medication.

A few years after their wedding, Marra had to stop taking her medication for a few months due to surgery. Kevin was suddenly faced with a woman who was like a stranger to him.

On her way up into her manic phase, she'd get as self-absorbed as a teenager. She'd take the car to get serviced and not pay any attention to what had been done. She'd wash half the dishes and leave the rest. Then, as she'd slide down into depression, she'd say mean things to Kevin. She'd be hostile and cutting.

Finally she was able to get back on medication, and he found again the woman he had married. But he was reserved and still hurting from the things she had said in her wild volatile state. He tried to talk about it, but she couldn't remember how she had been or the hurtful things she had done, so she couldn't really acknowledge or appreciate what he had been through.

Eventually he put it behind him and they settled into a comfortable marital relationship.

Then, on a holiday, for no special reason, she was suddenly spiteful to him. He found himself pulled into absurd arguments that went in circles. Then he realized Marra had run out of pills and hadn't bothered to refill the prescription.

These ups and downs continued for years. Kevin finally learned that the minute she went off the medication, he had to set boundaries. Only when she ran into consequences— consequences only he could establish—would she get herself back on medication.

After such episodes, she continued to have amnesia about her erratic behavior. Thus she had no idea that when she changed, his whole manner of operating also had to change. She literally did not know of the adjustments he made when she was not well.

Once, soon after she'd recovered from a relapse, he asked, "Did you feed the dog?"

She was offended. "Of course I did. Do you think I'm not a responsible person?"

He felt stymied. She didn't know that during her relapse, she *wasn't* a responsible person. It was lonely for him not to be able to talk to her about it.

When someone suffers from an emotional disorder that affects their thinking, behavior, attitude, or mood, sometimes the only thing that will save the situation—other than effective treatment—is boundaries.

Some people resist continuing with medication that lifts them into joy and life. Over and over again, I've watched certain clients fight medication, even though they are tortured mentally when they aren't using it.

If you are close to someone who needs medication but is

resistant to staying on it, you can set a boundary of not having contact with them when they are not in a healthy mental state.

This is done not to control the other person, but so you can determine the kind of experiences you allow into your life. You have the right to limit contacts that are hostile, abusive, or crazymaking.

Kevin found that setting boundaries was the one and only thing that would penetrate Marra's out-of-kilter states and jar her into realizing she needed to be taking her medication. Before he caught on to setting boundaries, he had turned himself inside out trying to talk to her, cajole her, encourage her, manipulate her, and monitor her into taking her pills. None of these worked. In fact, they all only fed her disease and increased her manipulation. Only when he stepped back and took care of himself did she come forward with a healthy response.

In my own practice, I've learned that when a client has a disorder that causes them to be manipulative, I do them a disservice when I allow their manipulations to work. Accepting manipulation only feeds the disease. In contrast, holding firm boundaries feeds and encourages the healthy person buried under the disorder.

And what if *you* have a disorder that causes you to lose your memory or mistreat someone you care about?

Don't hide behind your disorder or use it as an excuse. "Well, I only did it because I wasn't in my right mind." Remember that the other person still suffered, whether you meant them to or not, whether you could help it or not. They still were hurt because of how you acted.

Take responsibility for your behavior. Make amends for the hurt. Appreciate the gift the person gives you in choosing to hang in there and stay committed to the relationship.

Don't expect them to quickly and automatically become trusting again after you've recovered from a relapse. They can't simply push a button and feel safe again. Even if *you* can't remember what you've done, understand that it will take them awhile to learn that you are paying attention and being responsible again.

Sometimes, the best gift you can give the other person is simply to listen as they talk about their difficult experience. As you take responsibility for your own treatment and do what you can to be as healthy as possible, you will have a greater capacity to hear the other person's side without feeling a loss of self-esteem.

SETTING LIMITS

Most people will respond to consequences. By setting firm boundaries around the actions you will not accept, you can influence the course of your relationship with almost anyone.

Siobhan's mother had been self-absorbed all Siobhan's life. Now, eighty-six years old and afflicted with Alzheimer's, she was meaner than ever. Siobhan would pick her up every Monday and take her on an outing and to lunch. She would endure a continuous litany of complaints and criticisms and then take her mother back home.

She paid a terrible price for allowing herself to be abused. She felt bad about herself; she was bottled up with anger and grief; she hated Mondays; and she stuffed herself with sweets every Monday evening to help numb the pain.

Through counseling, however, Siobhan slowly learned to set boundaries with her mother. One Monday, as they drove toward the restaurant, her mother started in on her. Siobhan stopped her and said, "Mom, if you are going to continue criticizing me, lunch is out. I'll take you home." To her surprise and delight, her mother suddenly stopped her torrent of criticism.

They had a pleasant lunch together. Then at the grocery store an hour later, her mother made a cutting remark. Siobhan took her mother by the arm, left the basket, and led her from the store.

"What are you doing?" her mother cried.

Siobhan said, "I'm taking you home."

"Why?"

"You were rude to me."

"I didn't mean it."

"I'm still taking you home."

"I want to get some oranges."

"I'm taking you home."

By setting a firm limit and not accepting any excuses, Siobhan gained power over her emotional space. And her mother, despite her Alzheimer's, learned to stop criticizing her. Since any activity was immediately aborted the minute she became critical, she quickly stopped being critical.

(Can everyone with Alzheimer's learn or is this case special? As the brain deteriorates, one's ability to learn, process, and remember decreases. Still, I've been amazed at how people with all sorts of physical or emotional conditions will repeat a behavior that is rewarded and stop a behavior that costs them something they want.)

Never accept abuse. The cost is too high and the other person is never benefited.

Chapter 23

WHEN SOMEONE IS DYING

Even though we all know we'll be exiting this world, everything changes when we are given a rough idea of our time of departure. Our entire focus shifts, and we begin to see both life and death differently.

Each person approaches death uniquely. Most of us go through the stages of grief—denial, sadness, anger, depression, and acceptance—but we vary in the amount of time spent in each stage, and some people repeat the cycle at ever deepening levels.

In addition, dying people often face physical challenges. They may feel sick or in pain or be medicated. They could be dealing with loss of mobility, energy, or options. They may be faced with giving up their home, activities, work, or lifestyle.

Let the dying person set their own limits for how often and how openly the two of you discuss their death. But do make it clear that you're available for such a discussion.

"Gram, do you want to talk about this at all? I want to be here for you any way you need me."

"Aunt Jessie, if you have thoughts about dying or leaving

home, I'll listen. I care about you. You sure have been through a lot of changes."

If you need to convey your own feelings about the person's illness and death, let them pick the time. For example: "Carrie, could we have a little talk, sometime when you feel like it?"

Don't keep bringing up their death in casual conversation, however. When someone is dying, they usually try to get in as much living as they can. If they're drinking in the beauty of a rose, don't mention that it's probably their last summer. This is like drenching them in ice water. A tactless comment can interrupt their deep and rich living—and take them out of fully experiencing the moment.

Sarah was traversing her last fall. She loved the brilliant leaves of the maple tree outside her bedroom window. She noticed, though, that it seemed to be losing its leaves too quickly. One afternoon she saw her sister shaking the tree.

"What are you doing?" Sarah called in horror.

Maggie answered, "I'm raking leaves. I'm trying to get the leaves out of this tree so I can be done."

If you live with a dying person, don't be in a hurry to close off the seasons. Don't rush to put away holiday touches. Who cares if the Christmas tree stays up a few weeks longer? If your loved one is gaining pleasure from the beauty of a decoration, don't be confined by arbitrary time limits.

Be careful about making statements such as "You look great" or "You don't look sick at all." While someone concerned about their appearance can be reassured by such a comment, a different person might be insulted, as if you think appearance really matters, even though much more important things are happening. Yet another person might feel you are doubting their diagnosis or invalidating their dying process.

Be mindful about reporting the latest remedies you've heard about. We do this because we want to be sure a loved one has every opportunity for recovery. But by now the dying person is probably an expert on their disease. They probably know much more about it than you do, and they've likely been considering their options extensively. If they are finished weighing pros and cons and have already made the difficult decision about how aggressively to fight their condition, new information can be upsetting. If they are at peace with a decision, your well-meaning enthusiasm for a treatment you read about in a weekly magazine can be stressful. They may feel obligated to look into it when, in fact, they've already moved past the decision-making stage and are focused on something else. This could take them backward instead of forward.

Sometimes a death sentence can be a relief to someone who has had a hard life. It's permission to let go and quit trying. No matter how much we love that person, those of us on the outside must let them make the choice to die. We each have sovereignty over this basic issue. Lecturing someone on the ways they might fight to live can be a burden.

Some people do fight to live, of course. They want to know of every remedy, every research article, every smidgeon of information about their disease. That person will probably welcome what you've found. The simplest way to do the right thing is to ask. For example, "Do you want to know about the remedies that have helped other people with this problem?"

There's no easy way to lose someone you love, whether they go precipitously or by inches. Each aspect of loss hits us hard. Yet the way we choose to handle our feelings about our loved one can convey respect and protect them from further burdens.

• • •

As my beloved grandmother approached death, I wanted to be sure she understood what she meant to me. Yet to blurt out my feelings without considering her own ways and needs could have led to an unsatisfying experience for both of us.

She was of a generation of Midwestern women who didn't speak of feelings or of powerful experiences. She was accustomed to people who put a pleasant face on things, regardless of what was actually happening.

She departed slowly, over a span of years. It was hard to watch. Each time she lost a part of her life—when she no longer cared to be taken on car rides, when she could no longer talk on the phone, when I couldn't get her to eat—I felt fresh grief. Each loss hurt like fire.

I didn't ask her to help me process the grief I felt. I wanted to be mindful of what she was comfortable with. Thus I would mostly show rather than speak my love—by reading to her, or stroking her hand, or devising activities she'd be interested in.

Having said all this, it can be a great relief when two close people share their grief. For some people, putting a positive face on things can be a strain. If someone prefers to express their honest feelings, let them—in fact, encourage them to. Just by crying in each other's arms, we can be energized into another episode of living.

When the Dying Person Caused Harm

Mary's father had alternately terrorized and abandoned their family. If the cash was flowing from his factory job, he drank and beat her mother, Mary, and her two younger sisters. If he had been laid off, he drank till the money was gone, beat everyone, and went fishing with his buddies. Mary was fifteen when he was booted out of the factory for the last time for making an expensive mistake while under the influence. He took the family silver and the midnight train and disappeared.

Mary proclaimed good riddance, but her mother struggled. She worked her hands raw as a cleaning lady and got her girls educated enough to make a better life for themselves and then died from exhaustion. Mary's father missed the funeral and every other significant event from then on.

Mary grew up, married a man who didn't hit women, and raised a family. She was a generous, caring woman, but the fear planted by late-night howls and fists never left her. Fear kept her from taking the chances that would have let her study music and do something with a mellow honeyed voice. It kept her from adventuring into wild-river rafting in her mountain community, something she longed to try but couldn't risk. Fear enclosed her life like a Plexiglas cage and influenced all her choices.

Her father finally showed up—when he was dying from liver cancer and emphysema. He lay in the hospital and asked his daughters to succor him.

At one point Mary handed him a glass of water and in a fit of irritation, he hit her arm hard and sent the glass flying. I would probably have walked out at that point. Even if a person is dying, we still get to protect our boundaries. We do not have to give up our safety for the sake of a sick person.

Mary grabbed his wrist, leaned over, and got close to his face. "Do not strike me. Do not ever hit or slap me. Never again." Her tone was firm and quietly powerful. He never tried it again.

His life, however, influenced his death. His other daughters and their children wanted nothing to do with him and would not visit him. His lingering years were lonely ones.

Mary tried to talk with him about the things that had happened. It would have helped her healing if he could have said out loud that he had made their childhood home miserable. He wouldn't respond or acknowledge any of his acts. He wouldn't help her. She had to let go of the hope that he would turn into a loving and caring parent.

Close to his last days, she was able to sit with him. Just before he died, she said to him, "I forgive you." She was not through with her anger or grief at all that had happened, but she let him go spiritually.

She handled this process in an honorable way and kept good boundaries. She wouldn't let him abuse her. She didn't abuse him. She tried to talk about the things important to her. When he ignored her, she understood she would never get what she needed from him and protected herself by not continuing to try.

We keep ourselves stuck when we try relentlessly to get what another person can never give. To keep pushing for it violates both of us. The other is violated because an emotional limit is pummeled. We violate ourselves by putting our energy into a person who can't respond with what we need.

To forgive him released her in a spiritual way. It cut the cord of looking to him for completion of the broken matters between them. In some cases premature forgiveness cuts off the healing process, but this time, when she had tried to work out things appropriately, forgiving him set her free.

BOUNDARIES TO KEEP WITH A DYING ABUSER

- Do not harm them.
- Do not violate their boundaries. This will only pile up heavy costs for you.
- Do not let them violate you.
- Don't give more than you can afford to give.
- Don't sacrifice yourself, your time, your health, your family, or your financial security for the dying person.
- Find ways to approach getting what you need from the other in order to have closure. If the other is unable to respond, let it go after a reasonable try.

BOUNDARIES FOR SEEKING RESOLUTION

Do make an effort to discuss the things that have hurt you. Give it a good try. Find alternative ways to present the idea of talking things out. If they categorically refuse, ask if they'll consider talking later. (It's okay to bring up the idea of talking more than once, but let yourself know when it's hopeless to engage the other in an open discussion.)

If you can't get as full a discussion as you'd like, think about ways to get pieces of what you need. Sometimes a person can't talk about a whole series of abuses, but they can talk about one incident. Sometimes they'll resist a discussion with accurate words, but can stand a metaphorical conversation.

If the person in your life isn't capable of any level of honesty, at some point you'll protect yourself by letting go of the effort to get what they can't give.

Some dying people *want* to clean up their pasts. As death

approaches, the mists lift and some people can evaluate their errors with clarity. If this person wants to talk, expressing remorse for past harmful acts, let them. Listen. Some well-meaning relatives try to squelch the flow—"Oh, no, Pops. It's okay."

Don't make this mistake. Admitting wrong is a spiritually liberating process, and releases the injured person in a way nothing else can. An eleventh-hour housecleaning can free both people tremendously.

It's wonderful for the whole family to let light shine on the darkness. Considering how many years of harm are done by abuse, it's amazing how quickly healing spreads when the truth is told.

Chapter 24

AUTONOMY BOUNDARIES

After three weeks of intense work, Sunny finally completed a series of complicated reports required by her firm. She had been so consumed by the task that she had almost forgotten whether it was winter or spring.

As she turned in the reports, a lightness of heart floated her out of the office and toward her car. She couldn't wait to peer into Clint's face and catch up with him.

On the way home she pictured an evening of getting reacquainted with her husband. She planned to take him to a favorite restaurant and converse during a leisurely meal. Then she had a four-day weekend that was totally open. No kids coming, no parties scheduled—a lovely block of time for gardening, resting, and reading.

As she entered the house, he called out, "Oh good, you're here."

She started to respond with something equally affirming when he continued, "I need to take the car to the shop tonight. Follow me and pick me up."

As she trailed his taillights through the dark shiny streets into town, she still imagined having time with him at dinner. She watched as he parked the car and dropped the key through a slot into the closed repair shop. She enjoyed the sight of his easy lope toward her car. He eased into the seat beside her and said, "We need some things at Payback, and also food. How about you drop me off at the market and go on to Payback with my list?"

She took the list and dropped him at the all-night grocery, then headed on to Payback.

What was missing in this series of transactions?

- Some sort of acknowledgment of each other and the relationship before getting involved in tasks
- Sunny's voice
- Dinner

All of the above were missing, but I'm most concerned about Sunny's silence. Where did her voice go? Clint's needs were not urgent. He was dropping his car at a shop that was already closed. There was time for her to tell him what she had planned and to see if he'd be responsive.

As the weekend progressed, Sunny continued to make interesting decisions. Saturday was the day she usually attended her twelve-step meeting. She gave this up to play tennis with Clint, who had a passion for the sport. He loved having her with him, and it was a fun game. They each did chores in the afternoon and then went to a movie that night.

In Sunny's mind, Sunday was hers. That would be her day to needlepoint and watch old movies, one of her favorite combinations.

After breakfast on Sunday, she started stitching, but Clint wanted to watch the movie with her and asked her to wait.

She waited and waited for Clint to show up. Two hours later he settled into the couch, and she asked him what he wanted to see, even though she knew that she wanted to see a Cary Grant movie. He mentioned a historical movie and she said okay.

It was a two-part movie, but after the first tape, he said he needed to take a nap. He'd just sack out upstairs for thirty minutes. He asked her to wait till after his nap to watch Part II. She waited.

Three hours later he came back. By then it was too late to see the rest of the movie before the Academy Awards.

She felt resentful and irritated the rest of the evening.

What decisions did Sunny make that caused her to give away the weekend she had envisioned for herself? Can you mark the places in her story where she let her preferences slip through her fingers?

Sunny's decisions:

- To substitute tennis with Clint for her twelve-step meeting and time with friends
- To wait hours for Clint rather than set a time boundary or go ahead with her own desires when he didn't show
- To ask him what movie he wanted to see rather than tell him what she already knew she wanted
- To go along with his movie choice rather than negotiate the decision
- To wait for his nap to be over rather than go ahead with what she had wanted all along, or negotiate a resolution that met both their needs
- To continue to wait long after the thirty minutes he said he would need rather than either switch to what she wanted or tell him she wouldn't wait any longer

Her decision to skip the recovery meeting in order to have time with him could be a positive choice—but in this case, why couldn't they both have what they wanted? If she had said she wanted to play tennis with him and go to the meeting as well, couldn't they have met at the tennis courts after the meeting?

Throughout the weekend, Sunny withheld her ideas and preferences. Yet this was not an abusive marriage. Clint liked to be with her and was pleased when they shared things. He was not in a power struggle with her and didn't seek to control her. She deferred to him repeatedly when he didn't even ask her to. It's as if she forgot what she wanted as soon as he had an agenda.

Sunny also had a pattern of allotting time for herself only after she'd given everyone else what they wanted. She waited the whole three weeks of the reporting period before thinking of giving herself time with her husband. Then she gave time with him priority over time for herself. She gave him a treat by playing tennis with him instead of giving herself time with recovering friends—friends who might have helped her center herself and make better choices. She set the last day aside for herself, but then couldn't hang on to it, sacrificing bits of it for Clint's preferences.

Sunny did not keep boundaries around her own choices. She let them leak away. She kept giving away her autonomy by not using her voice. Such a simple thing can have big consequences.

Sunny lost more than a day of restoring herself. She lost the inner strengthening that occurs when we respect our own choices and protect the things we need to feel whole.

We are weakened when we don't allow ourselves the activities that refresh and restore us, and strengthened when we speak up about our preferences and are able to maintain the activities that re-create us. Autonomy means that we are self-directed, that we operate in the world from a place of independence.

OUR UNIQUE WAY OF DOING THINGS

Sonya had a method that let her mind be free for more important things. She would figure out the most efficient way to accomplish something, and then she would practice it till it was automatic.

She hated to search for her keys or her purse, so she put a hook by the door to the garage. She trained herself to hang up her purse and keys the minute she came home, and then she never had to think about it again. She had a series of routines that guarded her freedom of thought. The way she did laundry, cleaned, shopped, and handled money were all streamlined. This bought her extra time and the mental space to focus on her passion for designing gardens.

Naturally she married a random sort of person, a person who would put pliers in the same drawer as a deck of cards and plastic wrap, a person who would have glasses scattered in four different cupboards, and put cereal right next to crystal goblets.

Sonya didn't really notice the gradual escalation of Lang's disdain. His first jokes about Sonya's routines had a humorous edge. Over time, though, his remarks became truly insulting, and included words like *compulsive, anal, robotic.* She began to feel as if she was wrong to organize herself the way she did. She did go through certain steps before she left the house to shop, but on the other hand, she always had cloth bags with which to bring home the groceries, her bottles always got turned in for the refund, and they never had to eat alphabet soup for supper.

Despite the fact that Lang benefited from Sonya's routines, he often belittled her for them. She began to feel too rigid.

She tried to vary her routine, to be more flexible. He'd sit in the car honking and she'd run out without grabbing her coat or the list. Soon things at home got a little tattered. Sonya began to feel disoriented as she'd try to concentrate to make up for what she forgot. She stopped having time to pore over decorating magazines. Eventually her mind felt too dull to create.

What happened?

Sonya was a victim of a subtle type of abuse that sabotages autonomy and creates disorientation. She was attacked for her way of doing things.

We are each unique in the way we move through a day. One person follows a routine. Someone else acts spontaneously. One person is benefited by being organized. Another feels stifled by it.

Lana starts playing the minute she hits the weekend. Late Sunday evening she suddenly remembers to prepare for work and runs the laundry during the Sunday night movie. Ellen needs to get all her chores done before she can relax. On the way home from work she stops at the bank and the market. Saturday morning she cleans the house and does laundry, and then she's free.

We all have our own way of thinking as well. Nat thinks in a straight line. Bill thinks like a leapfrog. He is sometimes hard to follow, but he's usually entertaining—and he's often right on the money.

When someone targets our automatic processes, our way

of working, thinking, or handling life, we lose autonomy if we don't put a stop to it. By letting such abuse continue, we lose self-direction and emotional independence. Off balance, because we're trying to keep ourselves going with a process that's foreign to us, we can become disoriented and confused. We won't be as efficient, we'll make more mistakes, and soon we'll lose confidence in ourselves. This downward spiral leads to a progressive loss of inner direction.

The problem with this type of boundary violation is that it is so subtle. We are each so unconscious of our own processes. Our way of thinking and our way of organizing our lives are so natural and so much parts of ourselves that they are transparent to us.

Don't accept snide remarks about your way of doing things. Stand up for yourself if you are attacked or criticized for your individual processes (unless, of course, your way harms or gets in the way of someone). The point is not to convince the other person (who, by the way, is scapegoating you), but to give your own body and psyche the message that you will stand up for your way of being in the world.

If you're being not-so-gently teased, call the other person on it. Ask them to stop; possibly ask them about any anger or vexation that may be behind their teasing.

Are you the one who is likely to tease? Be sure that it comes from love or appreciation of their endearing ways. If you sense an undercurrent of anger, the teasing has an edge. Stop and look at yourself to identify the true reason for the anger. If it represents an issue with the other person, deal with it cleanly and directly. If it has nothing to do with them, but is some misplaced anxiety resulting from something else, make amends and ask for help with your anxiety.

Sonya caught on to what was messing her up, and she decided to set a boundary with her husband. She said, "Lang, I have my own way of doing things and it works for me. Stop making those snide remarks about my routines. If you can't see that my efficiency benefits you, that's too bad. But, regardless, I don't want you to make comments about my ways anymore."

"You're so sensitive, Sonya. I was just joking."

"I'm willing to protect my natural way of doing things. This is who I am. I have a limit here. I want you to respect it."

"You're blowing it out of proportion. What's the big deal?"

"I can see that you don't understand what I'm talking about. But whether you understand it or not, I won't listen to such remarks again. I'll leave the room rather than put up with it any longer."

"You are so controlling."

"That's it. I'm out of here."

"What about supper?"

"I intend to enjoy it somewhere else."

Lang reacted with one defense after another and didn't take responsibility for his boundary violations. But Sonya kept herself on track anyway. Eventually Lang created a negative consequence for himself.

When you set a boundary, stay with it. Some people change only when they run into a consequence. Let those natural consequences occur. Don't protect another person from the consequences of their disregard. Doing so can interfere with their own learning.

Chapter 25

FOOD BOUNDARIES

Trisha Donahey was at a professional conference for school-teachers. She had been in food addiction recovery for some years and had become an expert on her own body. She knew to the milligram her tolerances for various foods.

At the break, she bought a 7-Up and went out to the veranda for air. Another teacher came up to her. It took a moment for her to recognize an acquaintance with whom she'd shared many recovery meetings a decade earlier.

Almost immediately the teacher began talking about her own recovery program. She had joined a very strict offshoot of Overeaters Anonymous. She spoke of it with fervor, and Trisha responded with genuine gladness that the program worked so well for her.

This teacher kept doing something, however, that made Trisha increasingly uncomfortable. The whole time she talked, she stared at Trisha's 7-Up, and there was a hint of superiority in her tone and attitude, as if she were somehow more righteous because she wasn't drinking a soda.

I've been researching food addiction for nearly twenty

years. It's a complicated and difficult addiction about which most people have only a cursory understanding. If you are addicted to alcohol, any form of alcohol will trigger a series of addictive reactions, which will lead inevitably to dependence on the bottle. Similarly, crack cocaine is rapidly addictive to everyone who takes it into their bodies.

In contrast, food addiction dances around, wearing veils. To a person vulnerable to food addiction, sugar is likely to be addictive, but it isn't always. For years twelve-step advisers referred to popcorn as the perfect snack food, but it turns out to be addictive for many people. Proteins were previously thought to be completely safe, but now we know that for some people, certain proteins trigger enhanced appetite. A woman can be addicted to a particular food at the age of twenty and not have a problem with it at forty, or after having a baby, or after the onset of menopause. Although she is still a food addict, the particular foods that trigger a reaction can shift.

So why this chapter on food boundaries? Why highlight food addiction when there are so many other addictions?

No other addiction is so confusing and so misunderstood as food addiction. We can assume with easy accuracy that it would be unwise to offer an alcoholic a glass of wine, but we can't make similar assumptions about someone recovering from food addiction. An outsider can't know what is the best food choice for a recovering food addict.

We wouldn't encourage a recovering gambler to attend the church bingo game, but we'd push a compulsive overeater to join us at a buffet. People confuse eating disorder recovery with dieting, whereas they are very different processes.

Also, a remarkable percentage of people seem to think it's okay to comment about another person's food choices. We would rarely say, "You look atrocious in that shirt," but some people routinely make judgments about what another person is eating.

Food plays many roles in our lives. It is sustenance, yes, but much more than that. If we really want to spend time with someone, we share a meal. Food is often the central event of many occasions and holidays. Certain foods have religious significance; others are forbidden. We give food as a symbol of love. No wonder there are so many different boundaries we may need around food.

Food addicts aren't the only folks who suffer from self-appointed food police. People can be notorious for making family members' eating their business. Some folks will push food. Others will make judgments about whatever food another person chooses. And for a really mind-blowing experience, there are those who will criticize a person's weight while pushing second helpings at them.

Let's take a look at what this food busybodiness is about. Picture this.

A mother and her middle-aged daughter, Karenna, are taking a break from shopping and having lunch. The daughter orders a tuna sandwich, fries, and a cola. Mom orders half a sandwich and a green salad. When the meals come, Mom looks disapprovingly at her daughter's plate and says, "You aren't going to eat that, are you? French fries will make you fatter."

Which of the following reactions from Karenna is most likely?

1. "Oh, my gosh, I had no idea. Thanks, Mom, for warning me," and with that she jumps up, grabs her plate, and flings it across the room as if it were poison.

2. "I know. I know," she says with a defeated tone. She pushes her plate away, still hungry, but feeling too vulnerable to sup in the presence of her mother. Later, alone in her car, she goes through a drive-thru and orders enough for two construction workers.

3. She says nothing, but boils with anger, watching her mother pick at the salad and leave half of the half sandwich. Two hours later, she eats two candy bars and snaps at her husband.

4. She says, "Mother, my body is my business. If you comment again on my food choices, I won't have lunch with you for a long time."

The fourth reaction, of course, is an example of setting a good food boundary. Reactions two and three come close to how many of us would respond. When we are criticized for eating, we could be angry at the intrusion, or feel resentful, bad about ourselves, defeated, misunderstood, or victimized.

Is Karenna's mother likely to make her see the light and change her behavior? Hardly, and that makes me question the motives of people who continue to comment on someone's eating habits when they don't get reaction number one the first time.

If policing another's food were successful, I could see the value of it, but it almost always produces more eating, not less. In reality, Karenna's eating is a control issue for her mother. She is really seeking to control her daughter, and gets as much emotional mileage out of Karenna's perceived failure as she would from instant acquiescence.

YOUR BODY IS YOUR BUSINESS

What's an eater to do? If you run into a food Nazi, set a boundary at the first incident. In the unlikely event that it is an innocent boundary error from someone who really doesn't know any better, the sooner you educate that person, the sooner the rest of us will be safe. If a desire to control others is being disguised in sheep's clothing, it will soon emerge, and you can deal with it directly.

"Mother, I've asked you before, and I'm telling you now. Don't comment on what I eat. My choices are my business. The next time you make such a remark, I'm taking my food and moving to another table, and that will be the last time we have lunch together for a month."

"I'm only trying to help, Karenna. I don't know why you're making such a fuss."

"Tell me what you're hearing me say."

"That you get all upset if your poor mother simply tries to help you improve yourself."

"Try again. That wasn't it."

"That you'll stop one of the things I most enjoy, having lunch with you when we go shopping."

"And what action on your part will lead to me choosing to do that?"

"If I comment on what you order."

"Correct. Thank you for listening. Now, what department do you want to hit after lunch?"

Notice that Karenna never engaged with her mother's attempts to derail her; as a result, she kept her power. If she had fallen for any of her mother's traps, she'd have lost her footing. But she set a clear, strong boundary and kept to it, insisting on being heard.

Her mother couldn't give her the whole enchilada. Even when she grudgingly relayed what she knew very well was Karenna's request, she still had to put in a little "poor victimized me" comment. Karenna did well by continuing to press for overt confirmation of her boundary.

FOOD PUSHERS

What should you do if, at Thanksgiving, Aunt Mabel keeps pushing you to eat her candied sweet potatoes? You can simply set a boundary.

"Aunt Mabel, I just can't eat any more sweet potatoes. Thanks, though."

If your clear boundary is not respected, your next limit has to be more firmly set.

"Aunt Mabel, please stop asking. They are hard to resist, but any more wouldn't be good for me."

Or: "Aunt Mabel, listen to me. I choose not to have more sweet potatoes. Stop asking."

If you care deeply about Aunt Mabel, you might be willing to do more for her. Think about what the sweet potatoes—and your eating more of them—means to her.

- Is cooking the one way she shows love?
- Is Thanksgiving her happiest day, the day she steps out of a lonely life into the energy of the family?
- Is she just trying to give something to you because she loves you so much?
- Are her candied sweet potatoes her greatest life achievement, winning her accolades at the county fair and putting her on the map?

The following responses acknowledge Mabel's true intent without your having to stuff yourself with food you don't want.

- "Aunt Mabel, I love you so much. And I know you love me, but I can't eat another bite of your sweet potatoes."
- "Aunt Mabel, it's so fun to be here with you. I love Thanksgiving because we get to be together, but I can't eat any more sweet potatoes."
- "Aunt Mabel, you're so generous. You are always giving me something and trying to make me happy. Thank you for loving me so much. Believe me, I'm very happy being here with you and eating your great cooking, but I'm full."
- "These are the best sweet potatoes in the universe. I'm going to write NASA and suggest they send your sweet potatoes to Mars as our best offering to any other life-forms. But I can't eat another bite, thank you."

When you perceive the person's true intent, and are willing to acknowledge it, the symbol—food—becomes less important.

"Aunt Mabel, I love you to pieces, but if I eat more of those, I'm going to have to turn down your pie, and that would be the greatest Thanksgiving tragedy since the Indians taught Englishmen to smoke."

Aunt Mabel says, "Oh pshaw," waves a dish towel at you, and sits down with wet eyes. Message received and returned; relationship strengthened.

ETHNIC AND RELIGIOUS FOOD BOUNDARIES

What is sustenance to some can be sacred (or sacrilegious) to others. It is *always* inappropriate to challenge, insult, demean, or pressure someone who is eating a particular food (or a particular way) for religious or ancestral reasons.

Saul was faithful to the Jewish dietary laws of *kashrut*. For him they were part of an important spiritual connection. But other guys in his department at work saw him as extreme, and, though they never said anything anti-Semitic, sometimes they teased him about keeping kosher with too much attitude.

He kept to his inner compass and didn't let their comments in. He refused to engage in arguments about what he ate, and he would shake his head whenever they asked him mildly disrespectful questions about keeping kosher.

One day, they decided to pull a prank on him. When he was out of the room, they snuck a piece of ham into his sandwich.

At lunch, they watched him covertly to see what would happen. He tasted the forbidden meat instantly and spit it out.

From then on, he carried a lunch box with a little padlock. He considered his relationship with his co-workers forever broken.

Those men were lucky in that Saul was so filled with faith that he didn't seek retribution or feel hate for them. But he never trusted them again, and the extra help he had previously extended to them was withdrawn.

Chapter 26

INTERNET BOUNDARIES

I was working on-line with a client recently when an "instant message" suddenly arrived. The writer had apparently added my professional screen name to her buddy list (through which she could tell when I was on-line). I did not know who she was, so I asked. She ducked the question.

This immediately split us into different levels of vulnerability. My identity was known to her, but she was withholding her identity from me. I was not willing to engage in a conversation on that basis.

The Internet is a vast playground for many people. You can assume any persona you want, as if putting on a costume, and enter chat rooms and on-line games with no one the wiser. It can be fun to enter dimensions that would be closed to you in real life due to age, gender, mobility, or appearance.

When all the people in a chat room are anonymous, they are on equal footing. But when a stranger crashes a private chat room where friends are meeting, it feels as threatening as a burglar entering the house.

There has probably never been so boundaryless an environment as the Internet, and many of us have tasted its freedom. I can now research medical studies without leaving my home. I can work with clients anywhere in the world. A client can write me at midnight—when a crisis is happening—instead of waiting a week for an appointment.

We have created a world that is all mind, all thought. We travel instantly, without need of a body, to any pursuit that draws us.

But not everyone using the Internet is playing. Many of us use the bulk of our Internet time working. So if you send an instant message to someone, use the same courtesies as if you were calling on the phone. For example, "Hi, I'm Suni. Are you working? Are you free to talk?"

FORWARD FRENZY

Forwarded messages can be a blessing or a curse. When we first galloped on-line, forwarding was great fun. We passed jokes at the speed of light all over the globe. Now, so many forwards can arrive in a day that it's impossible to read them all.

You are not, of course, obligated to read them. You can treat them as junk mail and ditch them. Or you can set a boundary based on who sends them. (I have a tight group of friends whose forwards I read, not only because their jokes are usually both funny and tasteful, but also because I want to keep current on the culture of our community. Another friend is always on top of social issues. I read her forwards because it's like having a personal newsletter of important political events. Most other forwards I scan lightly.)

Tell correspondents if you would prefer not to receive forwards. Or tell them the type of forwarded messages you want them to send. "Send jokes, no sexual ones please." Or "Political info only. No jokes."

If someone does not respect your limit, you now know something important about the person, and can protect yourself accordingly.

A Forwarded Message Is Not Communication

A person I hadn't heard from in years recently reached me over the Internet. She said she'd like to renew our friendship via the Net. I was open to that and said so.

Then I received a string of forwards from her, no more personal information or any material on which to regrow a relationship. I suppose for some people a forwarded message seems like contact—and it is, in the mildest sense. However, a forwarded message is not personal. It isn't real communication from one human being to another.

In Internet relationships, it's easy to measure and maintain parity. If a person says they really want to stay in touch with you, and you hear from them twice a year, they are showing you that they want to do regular updates but don't want to get very involved.

If you are writing a friend weekly and they are responding every four months, you are involved to a different degree. You can mention it and discuss it, or you can settle back to the level of the other person's willingness.

One hard thing about all relationships is that the person with the least involvement is the one who sets the level of intimacy. If you want an intimate relationship with someone and that person wants a casual one with you, the relationship will be casual. You can invite, model, and request, but the bottom line is, if the other person wants less involvement, that's all they will offer you, no matter what you do. In fact, disregarding their boundary will cause them to back away even further.

A person's true level of interest becomes obvious on the Internet, because their behavior is all you see. I've compared people's behavior on-line with their behavior in the flesh, and have found that they are consistent in both milieus, but more obvious on-line.

In person we can cloak a lack of availability in flowery words and impressive gestures, but on-line, either a person responds or doesn't, acknowledges or doesn't, is capable of engaging in true conversation or isn't.

INTERNET BOUNDARIES

- Decide your limits about engaging with people who remain anonymous. In general, proceed slowly and with caution.
- Communicate your preferences regarding forwarded messages.
- Pay attention to a lack of parity in the people you communicate with. If you are getting more contact than you prefer, you can say so. If another person's involvement is much less than yours, you can e-mail that person about it, or pull back so that you aren't investing a lot of energy in them.
- Take charge of your own level of risk, both with known friends and (especially) unknown people.
- Notice when you are risking more or less than the other person, and decide what fits the level of relationship you want to have with them.
- Treat instant messages with the same courtesy as phone calls, asking if the other person is available for conversation.

Chapter 27

THERAPIST BOUNDARIES

Sylvia urged Maurice to come to therapy with her. He went, grateful to have discovered a woman who was so willing to put effort into their relationship. He entered the experience prepared to trust and respect the therapist.

Sometimes, though, he felt he was being pushed subtly in the direction of Sylvia's preferences. It was a flavor rather than any clear action that he could put his finger on—except that he sometimes left the sessions feeling that no one was on his side.

Finally he asked Samantha, the therapist, "Do you have any kind of relationship with Sylvia outside this office?"

Samantha laughed and directed the question back to Maurice. "Do you often have the feeling that women are ganging up on you?"

Maurice laughed too, and admitted that at times it did seem as if women belonged to an exclusive club that he could not enter.

Their therapy proceeded for another few months. Then, in the middle of an argument with Sylvia, she suddenly flung these words at him: "You're jumpy. Even Samantha said that you're like a flea on a griddle."

"I disagree. I know I sometimes get anxious, but it's in reaction to not knowing if I can count on—" He stopped mid-sentence. "What do you mean, Samantha said that? When did she say that?"

"After our book club meeting the other night."

"You and Samantha are in a book club together?"

"Yeah, what of it?"

"How long have you been doing that?"

"Oh, I don't know. Few years at least."

"You discuss me?"

"Well, we don't really discuss you," Sylvia said. "But you come up once in a while. Listen, I'm hungry. Let's get some dinner."

Maurice was angry and didn't want to go back to therapy with Samantha. His trust of their therapist had been shaken, but he realized Sylvia could have misrepresented something Samantha had said just to fortify her own position.

At the next session, he confronted them both. He found out they had been in a book club together for years, and that Samantha had indeed made some comments about him to Sylvia.

What therapist boundary violations can you spot in the above incident? Mark the acts that were trust violations committed by Samantha.

1. Samantha has a social relationship with Sylvia.

2. Samantha concealed this social relationship from Maurice.

3. Samantha talked about Maurice outside of their therapeutic relationship.

4. Samantha didn't reveal that she had discussed him with Sylvia—or the content of their conversation.

All four acts were therapist boundary violations.

I keep thinking there's no need for me to talk about therapist boundaries—then I hear another story about some therapist who grossly violates client boundaries.

So, to set the record straight, the following events are considered "off limits" for a therapist—including a psychotherapist, psychologist, psychiatrist, psychiatric social worker, counselor, doctor, and psychiatric nurse—and a client who are in a therapeutic relationship:

- Socializing
- Going out to dinner
- Having lunch
- Meeting for breakfast
- Going to a dance together
- Touching sexually
- Sexual innuendo
- Flirting
- Sharing the same weekly sports activity on the same team
- Repeatedly sharing a leisure activity together
- Taking a trip together, just the two of them
- Spending the weekend together, just the two of them
- Nourishing a friendship
- Going to parties together
- Having regular long talks on the phone in the evening
- The therapist being good friends with the client's spouse or partner

- The client being a good friend with the therapist's spouse or partner
- The client mowing the therapist's lawn
- The client cleaning the therapist's house
- The client providing a personal service to the therapist
- The client attending to the therapist's aging parents
- The client being the therapist's massage therapist
- The therapist becoming lovers with one of the clients in couples counseling

Why are these boundaries so strict? Because clients need the safety and scope of knowing that in the therapeutic relationship there exists a nested, private preserve all their own.

The therapeutic relationship is like a tunnel into the innermost tenderness of being. Here are found the ancient wounds that direct one's life. Here, at the fountainhead of fear or grief that influences choice and action, is therapeutic territory.

The therapist's office becomes the anteroom to that sacred tunnel, and the therapist becomes the guide. Over time, if the therapist is trustworthy, skilled, and aware (and if the client is willing), the client gains access to their soft inner self. The therapist teaches the client, through modeling and skilled interaction, how to receive buried and potent truths, and how to coddle their soul.

The focus of the client-therapist relationship is the client's inner self. It would be a rare client indeed—and a rare therapist, too—who could add any other kind of relationship to this delicate process and not (wittingly or unwittingly) sabotage it.

Adding a second role to the therapeutic one—sports buddy, friend, employer, or employee—inserts an interactional dimension that switches the focus of the relationship. The delicate internal journey that is therapy is challenge enough, without adding such complications to it.

The therapist can also suffer negative results by mixing relationships. The therapist may lose privacy, flexibility, or freedom of response. What if your client, whom you've hired to cut the grass, pulls as a weed the fifty-year-old clematis that your grandmother planted? What if, on the golf course, your client makes a smart-ass remark about your drive that pisses you off (and costs you three strokes)? What if your client botches a throw that loses the championship ball game? What if, at a party you are enjoying with your spouse, your client suddenly begins sobbing?

All sorts of sticky wickets are raised when a therapist and a client add some other type of association to an already complex, subtle, and potentially life-changing relationship. It is simply not comparable to being friends with your pediatrician, minister, or car mechanic (although even in these other professional relationships, mixing friendships can sometimes create some issues).

The most obvious boundary violation is anything sexual with a client. Why is this wrong? Because clients are vulnerable in a therapeutic relationship. They invest the therapist with trust. They are open at a deeper level than in ordinary social situations. A therapist who exploits this trust for sexual gratification is creating harm at a deep level. It's the same sort of violation as a parent using a child sexually. The person in the power position is stealing safety, ease, and trust from someone who is vulnerable. It is wrong.

So, if you have a therapist who puts the make on you, get away from that person quickly. Don't linger to teach the therapist proper conduct. Don't wait until you have enough evidence to sue. It's not worth the detour from your own progress. Leave that relationship immediately at the very first sexual action, and find someone else.

A good therapist has three attributes: ethically based boundaries, knowledgeable skill, and empathy. If any one of these is missing, you may get utilitarian sessions, but you'll miss out on the true potential of quality therapy. If it's the ethical aspect that the therapist is missing, you can be endangered. I know of no state board or educational program that prevents licensure due to moral emptiness, so it's up to you to protect yourself.

PASTORAL BOUNDARIES

People who have been trained as pastoral counselors are closely related to ministers. Their perspective is that of shepherds guiding their flocks. They consider their territory a person's whole life—family, home, work, social life. They are used to a context where people worship, break bread, raise children, play, pray, and learn together.

Even in this type of counseling, however, certain boundaries must be respected. In fact, because of the blended nature of pastoral relationships, boundaried behavior is even more important.

A pastoral counselor must be careful never to reveal secrets from one parishioner to another. Furthermore, since a pastoral counselor is in a far more extensive parental role than even a private therapist, sexual overtures toward a parishioner are completely out of bounds. (An exception would need to meet all the following conditions: the counselor and parishioner are both unmarried or unpartnered; the two have first established themselves as peers; the counselor is not involved in any sort of direct counseling with the parishioner or the parishioner's family; mutual consent.)

Psychotherapists, psychologists, psychiatrists, and pastoral counselors enter into a covenant when they accept a client. They agree to use their best resources on behalf of the client, keeping their personal needs out of it. These boundaries with the client help preserve the integrity of a vital, life-giving relationship.

The therapist-client relationship mirrors other relationships where one person is in the position of mentor, steward, authority, employer, or parent to another. Those with power have certain responsibilities toward the people they serve, assist, teach, supervise, or lead. The person who has power carries an ethical mandate not to exploit their position, not to abuse a subordinate in order to extract personal gain.

Therapist boundaries serve both to protect the client and to model clean, trustworthy authority. Thus, of all the boundaries we need, boundaries with therapists, counselors, and spiritual leaders are among the most critical—and can cause the most damage if they are violated. This is not only because the client or follower is open and vulnerable, but because, from the therapeutic experience, clients can envision the boundaries that apply to other situations in which they invest someone else with authority.

If it seems I've drawn these boundaries with a particularly heavy hand, it is because there is so much at stake. So much can be lost through even an accidental or well-intentioned violation.

By knowing about boundaries, you can make good judgments about whether or not a person deserves to be granted authority. When someone you look to as an authority behaves in a way that is beyond appropriate ethical limits, you can withhold your trust, withdraw your generosity or energy for the person, and even remove yourself from the relationship.

By preserving good boundaries, we can learn to look beyond titles to the standards a person keeps. Knowing the correct boundaries for any situation enables us to choose what our relationship with another person will be. Boundaries free us from the tyranny of roles.

Chapter 28

YOUR SAFE COUNTRY

A remarkable change can grow in your life as you practice the art of setting boundaries. Your life takes on more definition. You know who you are more clearly. Time and energy are freed for your chosen pursuits. People gain respect for you.

As you set clear boundaries in different situations, you may begin to discover yet another benefit. As boundaries knit together, we begin to have a clearer sense of our spiritual presence in the world. Although boundaries are a practice, a defined behavior, they also carry us to a wider place within ourselves, a place where we discover what our lives are really about.

Harbra grew up in a fractured family. Her alcoholic father's attention was on matters outside his family. Her mother, Cilla, was narcissistic and manipulative. Cilla's primary interest in her children was in what they could do for her. Harbra did an amazing job of taking herself out of the culture that raised her. She educated herself, got a good job, and entered therapy. Over time, she set clearer and firmer boundaries with her mother and her other relatives, but they still